The History of the Church and the Local Churches

Witness Lee

Living Stream Ministry
Anaheim, California

First Edition, 4,600 copies. May 1991.

Library of Congress Catalog
Card Number: 91-61860

ISBN 0-87083-579-3 (hardcover)
ISBN 0-87083-578-5 (softcover)

Published by

Living Stream Ministry
1853 W. Ball Road, Anaheim, CA 92804 U.S.A.
P. O. Box 2121, Anaheim, CA 92814 U.S.A.

Printed in the United States of America

CONTENTS

PREFACE

This book is composed of messages given by Brother Witness Lee in the spring of 1973 in Los Angeles, California.

CHAPTER ONE

THE HISTORY OF THE CHURCH

(1)

Scripture Reading: Matt. 20:25-28; 23:8-12; Rom. 14:1-3, 5-6, 17; Gal. 6:15; Eph. 2:15; 4:3, 14, 24

In this book we want to see how the Lord has moved in the past among His children for the accomplishment of His purpose. First, we want to see the history of the church in a general way, and then we want to see the history of the local churches beginning from 1922 (editor's note: this history was given by the author in 1973).

GOD'S GOAL—THE CHURCH

God's goal is the church, and the church is a corporate matter. The book of Ephesians reveals the church in seven major aspects: the Body (1:22-23), the new man (2:15), the kingdom (2:19), the household (2:19), the dwelling place of God (2:21-22), the bride, the wife, of Christ (5:23-32), and the warrior (6:10-20). These aspects of the church are all corporate matters. Throughout the centuries of church history, the problems, the confusion, and the divisions took place due to the saints not seeing the corporate church of God. In the past the saints saw something concerning such items as God's salvation, sanctification, and the need of being spiritual, keeping the holy Word, not loving the world, and being for the Lord's interest and work on this earth. They also saw that we need to labor to win souls and that we need to be enthusiastic for evangelism to the extent that we would go to other lands for the spread of the gospel. However, all of these items are not God's goal but are the means to reach His goal. God has only one goal. God's goal is unique. God's ultimate goal is the church.

The church is not something merely for the future. Today

is the dispensation, the age, of the church. The next age is the age of the kingdom of a thousand years. The church is for now; the church is for today. God's goal is to have a church today, a church in this dispensation, a church on this earth. Many dear saints throughout the centuries received light on many things in the Bible, but they missed the mark of God's divine economy and the goal of God's eternal purpose. The Lord desires to fulfill His purpose and to make His goal so clear to all His loving seekers.

THREE ITEMS WHICH DAMAGE THE CHURCH

The enemy Satan has used three main items to damage the church: Jewish religion, Greek philosophy, and human organization. These are the major sources of the church's division, ruin, and corruption. Because these items invaded the church, some of the faithful, living members of the church were burdened to defend the church, to keep the church away from Judaism, Greek philosophy, and human organization. These defenders were devoted Christians who loved the Lord, but they were not so clear about God's goal to gain the church as the corporate Body, the new man, the kingdom, the household, the habitation of God, the bride, and the warrior. Thus, although their intention was good, they made big mistakes in their defending of the church. In their intention to defend the church, some of them actually brought more damage to the church.

HIERARCHY BROUGHT INTO THE CHURCH

We can see an instance of this in the second century with a strong leader and defender of the church named Ignatius. Ignatius wrongly taught that an overseer, or a bishop, is higher than an elder. In Acts 20, however, Paul called the elders in the church in Ephesus bishops, or overseers (vv. 17, 28). The Greek word *episkopos* can be translated overseer or bishop. *Epi* means over and *skopos* means seer. The term *elder* denotes a person of maturity, while the term *bishop*, or *overseer*, denotes the responsibility and function of an elder. The responsibility and function of an elder is to oversee the church. From the erroneous teaching of Ignatius that bishops are higher than elders came the mistaken concept that elders are for a local church and bishops are for a region of churches. This led to the episcopal system of ecclesiastical government. This wrong teaching also became the source of the hierarchy of bishops, archbishops, cardinals, and the pope in today's Roman Catholic Church. Ignatius was able to make such a big mistake because he was not clear about the Body, the one new man. His erroneous teaching gave the ground to rank within the church and brought hierarchy into the church.

THE DEFENDING OF THE TRUTH
CONCERNING CHRIST AND THE DIVINE TRINITY

In the early days of the church, some great teachers stood up to defend the truth that Christ is both God and man. This was because Greek philosophy had entered into the church. When this philosophy became mingled with Christian teachings, it became known as Gnosticism, which taught that all matter is essentially evil. Those who held to the teaching of Gnosticism could not believe that Christ could have had the defilement of human flesh. Hence, they denied the incarnation, redemption, and resurrection of Christ. This is why the apostle John wrote that any spirit that does not confess that Jesus Christ came in the flesh is not of God (1 John 4:2-3).

The defenders of the truth attempted to clear up the different opinions concerning the person of Christ. This resulted in Christology, which is the study of who Christ is, the study of Christ's person. Arius was a heretical teacher who said that Christ was a creature but that He was not the Creator. The council assembled at Nicaea in A.D. 325 declared Arianism a heresy and rejected it. The Nicene Creed stresses that God is triune, that the Godhead has three persons—the Father, the Son, and the Holy Spirit. Many, however, unconsciously and subconsciously believe that there are three separate Gods. They do not understand that God is triune, not for doctrinal study or debate, but for the dispensing of Himself into His chosen and redeemed people.

Our God is the Triune God, and He has been processed so that He can be dispensed into us. For a watermelon to be dispensed into us, it must first be cut into slices. As we chew these slices, they become juice. The whole watermelon, the slices, and the juice may be considered as the "trinity of the watermelon." When the watermelon has been processed into juice, it can easily be taken into us to become our very element. God the Father has been processed through God the Son, and now He is God the Spirit. The Spirit today is like the juice of the watermelon available for us to drink. We all have been given to drink of one Spirit (1 Cor. 12:13). The Bible does not tell us that we have been given to drink of one Father or of one Son. We cannot drink the whole watermelon or the slices of watermelon, but we can drink its juice. Likewise, we can drink the Spirit, who is the ultimate consummation of the processed Triune God. Our God today is the "juice God." God has been processed.

The Divine Trinity was not fully revealed until the Lord Jesus was resurrected. After the Lord's resurrection, He came back to charge the disciples to go and disciple the nations, baptizing them into the name of the Father, of the Son, and of the Holy Spirit (Matt. 28:19). The Divine Trinity was never so clearly revealed as it was after the Lord's resurrection, because after His resurrection, God was fully processed. The "watermelon" has been fully processed to become the "juice." Because God has been processed, He is drinkable. The book of Revelation concludes with a call to take the water of life (22:17). The water of life is the processed God, the life-giving Spirit. Those defenders of the truth who wrote the Nicene Creed were not clear that the Triune God had been processed for the divine dispensing of Himself into His elect.

THE DIVISIONS OF CHRISTIANITY

As we have seen, due to the defending of the truth, different opinions were brought in among the so-called Christians. Then these opinions created great divisions. Eventually, western Christianity became the Roman Catholic Church, and eastern Christianity became the Greek Orthodox Church. Besides these two great branches of Christianity, there were the Nestorians in Persia. These were the three great divisions of so-called Christianity by the sixth century. Besides these three great divisions, there were many free groups. Because many free groups were breaking off from the general church, some designated the general church as the Catholic Church. *Catholic* means universal as one. Small free groups were formed because some Christians saw that the so-called general church had become worldly. They attempted to stay in the general church, but eventually they saw that there was no way to help it, so they began to meet by themselves. This happened again and again throughout the church's history. Again and again free groups were formed. The problem with all these groups, however, was that they did not see the corporate goal of God.

THE LORD'S RECOVERY

Some of us may feel that the Lord's recovery started with Martin Luther, but we need to realize that the Lord's recovery with His overcomers began in the second century. Within a short time after the completion of the divine revelation, the church fell into degradation, so there was the need of a recovery. The Lord's recovery began immediately after the degradation of the church came in. The line of the Lord's recovery started in the second century and has continued throughout the centuries.

Throughout the centuries those who loved the Lord would not go along with worldly Christianity. They desired to keep the Lord's word as much as they could. They desired to live with a pure conscience and worship God according to what they saw from the Scriptures. But I have to stress again and again that they were not clear about God's corporate goal. This is why the Lord's coming has been delayed even to this day. Regardless of how many groups of Christians there are on this earth, as long as there is no proper church life, the Lord does not yet have His goal.

We need to have the realization that we are the "church people." Day by day we are "churching." Churching is our work. We are the church. We are not denominational, interdenominational, or non-denominational. We are the church people. We are in the recovery of the Lord's goal. This recovery is not the recovery of justification by faith, salvation, or sanctification. We are in the recovery of the church, which includes the recovery of all the foregoing items.

THE FORMATION OF STATE CHURCHES

The Lord's recovery took a definite form with Martin Luther's stand for the truth concerning justification by faith. Luther was a great defender of salvation, of justification by faith, but he also made some big mistakes. On the one hand, he defended the truth. On the other hand, he made the mistake of becoming affiliated with the German government. This affiliation with the government was the source of the so-called state churches, or national churches. Do not think I am criticizing Luther. I realize that we all are human. On the one hand, we can be used by God to a great degree. On the other hand, we can be weak in other areas. Luther was strong for justification by faith even at the cost of his life. In his stand for justification by faith, he stood against the pope, the greatest power on earth at that time, but when he came to the question of the church, he was weak. This is according to the historical record. The first state church was the state church of Germany. Then many other European nations followed Germany such as Denmark, Norway, and Sweden. Eventually, the state church of England, the Anglican church, was formed. The Church of England is mingled with the government of England. Even today the queen of England is the head of the Church of England. The king of Denmark is the head of the Lutheran state church of Denmark, and the king of Sweden is the head of the Church of Sweden today. This came from Luther's mistake. Even Luther himself admitted that he was weak in this point. All the defenders of the truth made some mistakes. There is hardly one exception to this. All these mistakes were due to one great lack—the vision, the proper unveiling, of God's goal. God's goal is the church. By the Lord's mercy, the vision of the church, the revelation concerning God's corporate goal, is so clear today. We all need to be clear about God's unique goal—the church.

OUR SAFEGUARD AND BALANCE
BEING THE VISION OF THE CHURCH

According to my feeling, Brother Watchman Nee has been the greatest gift that the Head of the church has given to His Body, especially in this century. I can also testify to you for him from my pure conscience that he was also a great defender of the truth concerning the church. According to my knowledge, Brother Nee did not make mistakes because he was so clear about God's corporate goal—the church. As long as we have the vision of the church and are so clear about God's corporate goal, we are safeguarded. The church, the Body, the new man, the corporate goal of God's eternal purpose, is our safeguard. No matter how much we know the Bible, if we do not know the church, we will eventually make a serious mistake. If we are clear about the church, we are safeguarded. Nothing safeguards us so adequately as the knowing of the church, as the seeing of the Body. The Lord's recovery is ultimately for the church life. All the foregoing items of the Lord's recovery—such as the recovery of justification, sanctification, the inner life, and the proper understanding of prophecy—are for the present recovery of the church life. Today we are here for the church life. If we have really seen the vision of the church and that God only cares for the church, we will never be divided by any doctrine.

After the reformation with Martin Luther stressing justification by faith, the state churches eventually became empty and dead. The reaction to the deadness of the reformed churches was among the mystics who were still in the Catholic Church. The Lord raised up a group of people that included Madam Guyon, Brother Lawrence, and Father Fenelon. They did not care for the outward practices or teachings but only for the reality of the inner life. These saints, who were known as the mystics, were the start of the recovery of the living reality of the inner life. Their experience of Christ as the inner life began as a reaction to the emptiness of the reformed churches. However, the mystics, whom the Lord used for the recovery of the inner life, also made some mistakes because they did not see the

Body, the church. They did not have the safeguard of the Body and the balance of the Body.

We need to be impressed deeply that the safeguard of our whole Christian walk and the balance of our Christian life is the church. If we have seen the church, we will never be divided by anything. If we are clear concerning the vision of the church, we will never have hierarchy. For one to place bishops above elders indicates that he has not seen that the church is a living Body, an organism. The church cannot be controlled by human organization. Hierarchy is human organization.

Because the church is the organic Body of Christ, it can have nothing to do with organization. If something is wrong in our physical body, it is healed organically. The body is an organism. It cannot be touched or dealt with in an organizational way. The church is an organism. The church is not only the Body of Christ but also the new man. Just as the life within our physical body takes care of sicknesses, the life within the Body of Christ can take care of any problem. If there are some problems in a local church, it is best if we keep our hands off of these problems and leave them to Christ, the heavenly doctor. He is the life in the Body. We need to let the life in the Body work within the Body. Our own doing apart from this life is organization, and this will not help the Body but damage the Body. When we see problems in the church, we need to learn to hold back our being and our doing.

Every problem and trouble in the church is a temptation to the leading ones. If the leading ones in the churches hold themselves back when there is a problem, that is a great victory. The biggest temptation to the leading ones in the churches is the troubles and problems in the churches. They may feel that they have to do something to solve these problems. While we are doing something, however, we can be in the realm of organization, which damages the Body. We need to restrain our doing and let the life in the Body take care of the troubles and the problems. If we do this, it means that we know that the church is not an organization but the organic Body of Christ. If a person cuts his finger, he may need to take care of it in a proper way. But if he takes care of it improperly, he will do more damage to it. Eventually, the cut on his finger will be healed by the life within his body. The church is not an organization but an organism. Church history has shown that organization has damaged the church.

We all need to see what the church is. If we see the church as the corporate goal of God, whatever we do will be profitable to the Body. Because the defenders of the truth in the past lacked the proper knowledge of the church, they made mistakes that damaged the church. Today in the Lord's recovery we need to see the church, to see the Body. Then whatever we do will be a profit and will never be a loss or a damage to the church. The vision of the church is our safeguard and balance. As long as we stand with the church, we are safe. If we stay away from the church, we are in danger of damaging the church. May the Lord be merciful to us that we may see that opinions, organization, rank, and different teachings damage the church life. This damage takes place because people do not have an adequate vision of the church. Today in the Lord's recovery, the Lord desires to show us the ultimate goal of His purpose—the church life.

CHAPTER TWO

THE HISTORY OF THE CHURCH

(2)

Scripture Reading: Gal. 1:13-16; Phil. 3:5-8; Col. 1:18-19; 2:2-3, 6-10; 3:10-11

I hope that we can take some time to pray-read the verses in the Scripture reading at the beginning of each chapter (especially chapters one and two), so that we can be deeply impressed with them. I believe that these verses are very revealing and enlightening. If we are deeply impressed with them, we will see what the real church life is. These verses can convey to us a complete and clear vision of the church.

NO HIERARCHY IN THE CHURCH

In Matthew 20 and 23, the Lord Jesus told us clearly that among His disciples there should not be any kind of human rule or human position. Although the Epistles reveal that the elders are the leading ones in the churches (Heb. 13:7, 17, 24), they are not taking the lead according to the human, worldly way. The elders are not leaders in a positional or hierarchical sense. They have to be the examples, taking the lead to follow the Lord's way, and they should not exercise any lordship over the church. This is clearly taught in 1 Peter 5:1-3 and 1 Timothy 3:1-7. We should not be under the influence of the worldly understanding when we talk about leadership in the church. In the world the leaders have authority over others and rule over others. In the churches, the elders are the leading ones, but they are not rulers. They should be examples, taking the lead to serve and care for the church so that the believers may follow in the same way.

The elders also function to take oversight. We pointed out in chapter one that the Greek word for *overseer* is *episkopos*. *Epi* means over and *skopos* means seer, implying view or sight. The elders should function to look into the situation of the church with an overview. Perhaps some in the church would go astray or would bring in sinful, worldly things that would insult the Lord. Then the elders have to do something to keep the church in the Lord's way. We should not consider the elders as worldly rulers. They are only the examples, taking the lead to follow the Lord's way, and the saints should follow their example. The elders are also overseers who take the oversight in the church. They are watching to keep anything sinful or idolatrous from being brought into the church.

I want to stress that there should not be any rank or position in the church. Any hierarchy in the church is abominable to the Lord. It is a shame that those in the Catholic Church call their priests "father." In Matthew 23:9-10 the Lord said, "And do not call anyone your father on the earth; for One is your Father, He who is in the heavens. Neither be called leaders, because One is your Leader, the Christ." If we want to be great, we should be a servant, a bond slave (v. 11). The greatest one among us is our slave. Are we willing to be slaves to the brothers and sisters? We need to be slaves, serving the brothers and sisters and ministering Christ to them. Matthew 20:25-28 and 23:8-12 are very important portions of the Word. Based upon these two portions of the Word, there is no ground for any kind of hierarchy or clergy in the church. The Lord said that we are all brothers (23:8).

NO RELIGION IN THE CHURCH

We also need to be aware of religion invading the church. In Galatians 6:15 Paul said, "For neither is circumcision anything nor uncircumcision, but a new creation." According to the context of this verse, circumcision refers to religious ordinances and uncircumcision refers to being without religious ordinances. Neither of these mean anything. What matters is the new creation. The new creation is Christ with the church. Circumcision is an ordinance of law; the new creation is the masterpiece of life with the divine nature. We should be those who live in the reality of the new creation apart from any religious ordinances. In the past some cared for religious ordinances. We should not repeat the mistakes of the past. The failures of the past should be warnings and lessons to us. We should only care for the new creation, which is Christ with the church and the church with Christ.

CHRIST ABOLISHING ALL THE ORDINANCES FOR THE CREATION OF THE ONE NEW MAN

Ephesians 2:15 tells us that on the cross Christ abolished in His flesh the law of the commandments in ordinances to create the one new man. The new man is the new creation. Christ has abolished all the ordinances, including circumcision, the keeping of Sabbaths, and the dietary regulations of the Old Testament. All the ordinances have been abolished by Christ on the cross for the creation of this new man.

CARING FOR THE ONENESS OF THE SPIRIT AND PUTTING ON THE NEW MAN

We also have to remember Ephesians 4:14, which tells us that we should no longer be babes tossed by waves and carried about by every wind of teaching, or doctrine. Any teaching, even scriptural, that distracts us from Christ and the church is a wind that carries us away from God's central purpose. We should not care for distracting doctrines but care for the oneness of the Spirit (v. 3). We should also be those who are always putting on the new man (v. 24).

RELIGION PERSECUTING THE CHURCH

Galatians 1:13 reveals that when Paul was in religion he persecuted the church of God excessively and ravaged it. This shows us that as long as we hold on to something religious, we will be a persecutor of the church. Our religion is a persecution to the church. To some, *religion* is a positive word, but to those of us practicing the church life, it is a negative word. Religion is a damage to the genuine church life. If you are in the church, you are outside of religion. If you are in religion, you cannot be in the genuine church life. As we have pointed out, the church is an organism. The Body of Christ, the new man, is not a religion, even the most scriptural religion. The church is an organism as the Body, the new man, the kingdom of God, the family of God, the dwelling place of God, the wife of Christ, and the warrior fighting the battle. Religion persecutes the church, and religion is versus Christ. Paul was so zealous in religion, but it pleased God to reveal Christ in this one who was so advanced in religion. God rescued him out of the religious world by revealing His Son in him (vv. 4, 15-16a).

COUNTING ALL THINGS REFUSE TO GAIN CHRIST

In Philippians 3:5-6 the basic elements of being religious are mentioned. Paul told us that all these religious factors which had been a gain to him were counted a loss by him on account of Christ (v. 7). He also counted all things to be loss and even refuse that he might gain Christ (v. 8). "Refuse" in verse 8 is dregs, rubbish, filth, what is thrown to the dogs; hence, dog food, dung. Everything, including worldly things, fleshly things, and religious things, was counted as dung by the apostle Paul. To him everything other than Christ was dung. He counted everything as a loss that he might gain Christ. Anything that is not Christ Himself or that is a substitute for Christ, we have to count as dung. It does not matter whether that item is good or bad. As long as it is not Christ and as long as it is a substitute for Christ, it is trash. We should not bring anything other than Christ into the church. The church is not a trash can. Instead, the church is the new man and the habitation of God. In the church, nothing counts but Christ. Everything other than Christ is trash. This revelation is according to the holy and pure Word of God.

In Philippians 3:2 Paul said that we need to beware of the dogs. Dogs refer to the Judaizers, the religious ones. Paul said that he counted all things as refuse that he might gain Christ. Refuse is dog food. At one time Paul was a dog feeding on dog food, but then he became a member of Christ feeding on Christ. Only Christ is the real food. Anything other than Christ is dog food. All the worldly and the religious people are feeding on dog food. Only the proper church people are feeding on Christ. We need to be those who are feeding on Christ as the heavenly bread of life.

THE REVELATION IN COLOSSIANS 1—3

We also need to see the revelation presented in Colossians 1—3. Chapter one tells us that Christ is the Head of the Body (v. 18). As the Head of the Body, He must have the preeminence, the first place, in the church and in all things. He should have the preeminence. Chapter two tells us that Christ is God's mystery (v. 2). Whatever God is, whatever God has planned and purposed, whatever God has accomplished, and whatever God intends to do are altogether embodied in Christ as the mystery of God. In Him dwells all the fullness of the Godhead bodily (v. 9), and all the treasures of wisdom and knowledge are hidden in Him (v. 3). Christ is such a wonderful One. We cannot analyze Him or systematize Him. Christ is so marvelous, mysterious, and profound. We should not try to analyze Him because we cannot understand Him in full, but we can receive Him.

Colossians 2:6 says that as we have received Him, we should walk in Him. Verse 8 says, "Beware that no one carries you off as spoil through his philosophy and empty deceit, according to the tradition of men, according to the elements of the world, and not according to Christ." Philosophy here refers to the teaching of Gnosticism, a mixture of Jewish, Oriental, and Greek philosophies, which is an empty deceit. The source of the Gnostic teaching at Colosse was the tradition of men, depending not on the revealed writings of God but on the traditional practices of men. The elements of the world refer to the rudimentary teachings of both Jews and Gentiles, consisting of ritualistic observances in meats, drinks, washings, asceticism, etc. We have to beware of this today. We should not receive or walk according to any worldly philosophy, worldly teaching, or any kind of worldly natural thought. We should walk only according to Christ. We have to walk in Him and according to Him because all the fullness of the Godhead dwells in Him bodily, and we have been made full in Him (v. 10). Outside of Him, we will be empty, but within Him, we will be full.

According to Colossians 3:10-11, we have to realize that the new man, the church life, is upon us. It has been put on us, and now we have to practically put on the church life, the new man. In this new man "there cannot be Greek and Jew, circumcision and uncircumcision, barbarian, Scythian, slave, freeman, but Christ is all and in all" (v. 11). Circumcision refers to religious people, whereas uncircumcision refers to unreligious people. A barbarian is an uncultured person, and Scythians were considered the most barbarous. In the new man there is no possibility, no room, for any natural person. There is only room for Christ. Christ is all and in all. He is all the members of the new man and in all the members. He is everything in the new man.

THE CHURCH BEING COMPLETELY APART FROM RELIGION, PHILOSOPHY, AND HIERARCHY

I want to point out again that the church is completely apart from religion, philosophy, and hierarchy. We need to understand what religion is. Religion is worshipping God, serving God, and doing something for God without Christ as the Spirit. What we do may be quite good, fundamental, and scriptural, but if what we do is without Christ as the life-giving Spirit, that is religion.

There also should be no philosophy in the church. Philosophy refers to the human thought, the human concept, and the human understanding which is embodied in the human opinion. This philosophy is always expressed in different doctrines. Doctrine can be a cloak to human opinion. Something may appear to be a scriptural doctrine when actually it is the expression of a person's thought, opinion, or Christian philosophy. It can actually be one's self-made philosophy under the cloak of scriptural teachings.

We have to be careful not to use our mind apart from the Spirit. We need to be afraid of our natural concept, thought, and understanding. The natural understanding is really poisonous. In the churches the most blessed persons are the simple ones. The ones who are not blessed are the ones who are so much in the exercise of their natural mentality. We need to realize that our mentality is the ground where the tree of knowledge grows to produce all kinds of fruit of knowledge.

Ephesians 4:14 warns us not to be carried about by every wind of teaching in the sleight of men, in craftiness with a view to a system of error. The dividing teachings are organized and systematized by Satan to cause serious error and thus damage the practical oneness of the Body life. Satan utilizes the Bible teachings to systematize people and to bring them into systematized error. We have to be aware of the natural concepts and thoughts behind the winds of teaching. This means we have to reject the philosophies of men and the teachings that distract us from Christ and the church.

Furthermore, we should reject any thought or practice of rank and position in the church. Rank and hierarchy come from the struggle for power. If a brother is an elder, he should not have a pleasant feeling when people call him an elder. It is not so good to call a brother an elder. We want to avoid any concept of rank within the church. The term elder is not and should not be a title. We do not have the title elder among us, but we have some persons who are elders. We do not have any positions or titles in the church. We have to hate hierarchy (Rev. 2:6). That is an insult to Christ. It is a shame that clergymen are referred to as "reverend." Only Christ is reverend. Only He should receive our reverence. In the church there should be no religion, no philosophy, no vain doctrines or teachings, and no hierarchy, clergy, rank, positions, or titles. All the problems, confusion, and divisions come from these sources.

THE NEED FOR A VISION OF GOD'S GOAL—THE CHURCH

All the negative things we have mentioned crept into the church throughout its history. Some of the saints fought against these things and defended the truth. Ignatius, a great defender of the truth, was martyred at the beginning of the second century. We have seen that although Ignatius was such a defender of the truth, he made a mistake because he was short of a clear vision, a complete view, of the church. Nearly all the defenders of the truth made mistakes for this reason. Ignatius made a great mistake that turned into the

establishment of the episcopal system. He did it unintention-
ally. His heart was good, but he made a mistake because he
did not have a clear vision of the Body.

By the end of the sixth century, the papacy was fully
formed and established. During the five and a half centuries
before the establishment of the pope, many so-called puritans
were raised up by the Lord to fight for the truth. They loved
the Lord, loved the Bible, and stood for the Lord according
to what they had seen, but nearly all of them made some
mistakes. In the second century the term *Catholic Church*
was used. The so-called Catholic Church became very worldly.
Some of the faithful saints did not agree with this, and they
fought against the worldliness in the Catholic Church. This
was very positive, but they did not have a clear vision of the
Body. They were just for not being worldly. They were fighting
against worldliness and stood so much for not being worldly.
In a sense, that was good, but in another sense, they made
a mistake in that they became a mere free group of unworldly
Christians. They did not care for the Body, the church, the
new man, or for the oneness. They did not care for God's goal
but only for not being worldly. There are many Christians
today who are acting in the same principle of caring for other
things besides God's goal.

According to church history, human power, human rule,
hierarchy, and human organization crept into and prevailed
in the so-called church, but there was not much place or
ground left to the Holy Spirit. A group of puritans were raised
up who were very much against this. They declared that
the church should be under the authority of the Holy Spirit,
and they fought against human rule in the church. Regretfully, however, they did not care for the Body. They only
cared for being spiritual.

The first group I mentioned cared for not being worldly,
and the second group cared for being spiritual. However,
neither group cared for the oneness. They did not care for
the Body. Eventually, these kinds of free groups gave up the
Catholic Church, the general church, and began to meet by
themselves. History tells us that these groups even began to
exclude one another. They left the Catholic Church for

reasons and they stressed different points, and sadly they began to exclude one another. They became different free groups who did not receive one another.

Today's situation is not much different from what happened in the past history of the church. Some free groups are just for the study of the Bible. Others are for spirituality. Although these things are good, they are not God's goal and should not be an excuse to form divisions. Church history shows us that the so-called church in a general sense became degraded and that those who loved the Lord, who loved the truth, and who loved the Bible did not receive a proper, adequate, clear, and complete vision of the church. Although they defended the truth, they made mistakes that resulted in more division in the Body of Christ. Thus, it was difficult for the Lord to find vessels to carry out His purpose. This is the reason that the history of the church is generally a sad story.

If we do not have the vision of God's goal, we will be happily content with many revivals. One of the most prevailing revivals in the history of the church took place in Wales in 1904 and 1905. One story speaks of all the theaters in Wales being closed and of no one going to any worldly entertainment on Sunday. All of the people went to church meetings. But it did not last too long. It was only a revival; not much was accomplished for the fulfilling of God's eternal purpose, that is, the building up of the Body of Christ. That revival was wonderful, but we also need to consider what was carried out through it. Revivals are very positive for bringing people to salvation, but there is not much result for the fulfilling of God's eternal purpose.

We have to be clear what we are here for. We are not here merely to be separated from the world. We are not here merely to be spiritual. We are not here for revivals, mission work, or the study of the Bible. We are here for the Lord's recovery of the church. By His mercy, we have to defend the revealed truths in the Bible, but in our defending we should not make mistakes that will damage the Lord's Body. The way to be kept from making any mistakes by our defending is to take care of the church. Surely we should not be worldly and surely we have to be in the Spirit. The church should have no religion, no vain teachings, no philosophy, no human organization, no clergy, no hierarchy, no worldliness, no human power, and no flesh. But we should not defend anything of God's kingdom by making serious mistakes. In order for us to be safeguarded from making any mistakes in defending something of God's interest, we need to see the church.

PRACTICING THE CHURCH LIFE
BY BEING STRONG AND RICH IN THE SPIRIT

Some young people among us have really been saved and they are members of the church. They are members of the Body in actuality, but according to their outward appearance they do not express much of Christ. They need some time for transformation. Perhaps some would like to "protect" the church by not receiving young people who are "hippies." By doing this we make a big mistake. If we have this thought or would do this, we have never seen what the church is. This does not mean that the church should be loose or worldly, but the church should not regulate people's outward appearance. Both ways are wrong.

In order to practice the proper church life, we have to be in the Spirit, be strong in the Spirit, and be rich in the Spirit. Eventually, we will be neither loose nor outwardly regulated. Christ as the reality will be within us in a living, inspiring, revealing, subduing, and conquering way. Then the church will be neither loose nor demanding. Although the doors of the church are open to receive everyone, negative persons will be subdued. Some negative persons may come in among us, but eventually they will be subdued or they will go away.

The church is not a worldly organization or a human society. The church is something of life with power and impact. The elders should not regulate the church outwardly, but they need to get themselves sevenfold intensified with the Spirit. Then there will be neither outward regulation, nor outward demanding, nor any looseness. The church life will be full of liberty, yet there will be the demanding from the inner life and the inner control of the Holy Spirit. When some come in among us, they will either be convinced, subdued, captured, and wrecked, or they will stay away.

In these messages I do not have the intention of giving a detailed history of the church. My burden is that we would pick up some lessons so that we would learn not to repeat the mistakes of this sad history. We do not care for religion, philosophy, vain teachings, natural opinions, human authority, human organization, rank, position, hierarchy, or clergy. We do not agree with anything worldly, anything of the natural life, or anything fleshly. Although we do not agree with any of these negative things, we would not use any rules to regulate or to demand in an outward way. Then what should we do? We need to go to the Spirit to be burned and intensified with the sevenfold Spirit (Rev. 4:5; 5:6). Then we will have something living and burning with the impact, with the power, and with the way to minister the riches of Christ to people. There is no need for us to be anxious about guarding the church or watching over so many negative things. We believe that the power, the reality, the weight, and the impact of Christ as the life-giving Spirit is with the church.

CHAPTER THREE

THE HISTORY OF THE LOCAL CHURCHES

(1)

Scripture Reading: Rom. 16:17-18; Gal. 1:6-7; 2:3-5; 5:10b-12; Phil. 1:15-18; Col. 2:8

If any saint of the Lord is faithful to all the verses from the Scripture which we are pointing out in this fellowship, he will be in the proper church life. By the Lord's mercy, we have learned the truth of these verses over the past fifty years. The putting together of these verses comes from many years of experience, so I would encourage us to pray-read them again and again until we get into them and they get into us. These verses can be considered as the controlling verses of the ministry over the past thirty years. The Lord's ministry always focuses on Christ and the church.

REACTIONS AND DIVISIONS

We have seen that not too long after the church came into existence, the Lord's enemy, the subtle one, brought in three items to damage the church: religion, philosophy, and organization. We have to be on guard against these things creeping into the church because they damage the church to the uttermost. All kinds of evil things go along with religion, philosophy, and human organization.

Throughout all the centuries, there have been so-called puritans who always reacted to the impurities and negative things brought into the church. All the puritans were good in their intention to get into God's reaction to the degradation of the church, but because they were not so clear about the church as God's eternal goal, they made some serious mistakes. The biggest mistake made by them was that their reaction issued in more division. Whenever there was a reaction through the puritans, there was nearly always a division. Actually, nearly every reaction became a division. Reaction after reaction meant division after division. Eventually, God's goal was damaged. This has been the main reason that the Lord has not yet returned. He could not return because there was nothing for Him to come back to. In order for Him to come back, He needs a "stepping stone." This stepping stone is the proper church life that prepares the church as the bride for His coming. Even though there have been thousands and thousands of real believers, there has been a shortage of the proper church life. In all the reactions to the degradation of the church since the second century, there was not much accomplished for fulfilling the Lord's purpose to have the practical expression of the church.

THE RECOVERY OF JUSTIFICATION
BY FAITH WITH MARTIN LUTHER

At the time of the reformation, the Lord's recovery came into a definite form. Martin Luther was a great servant of God. The Lord used him to recover the truth concerning justification by faith and to make the Bible open to the general public. Thank the Lord that justification by faith has been fully recovered. It will never be lost again. At the cost of his life, Luther stood for this truth, but when he came to the truth concerning the church, he was weak. He did not bring us back to God's genuine intention to have the church life.

Luther realized that it was wrong to be joined with the German government, yet he still did it. Due to this big mistake, the state churches were produced. Besides the Roman Catholic Church and the Greek Orthodox Church, there are also the state churches. All the state churches are Lutheran churches except the Church of England, which is an Episcopal church. The German state church, the Danish state church, the Norwegian state church, the Swedish state church, and the Anglican state church were the issue of the seed sown by Luther. I respect Luther as one of the great servants of the Lord, but his mistake shows us that if we are short in our vision and knowledge of the church, we will have no safeguard. We may do the best thing and still make some mistake. Our safeguard is to know the church in an adequate way.

THE RECOVERY OF THE EXPERIENCES
OF THE INNER LIFE WITH THE MYSTICS

History tells us that the reformed churches, especially the state churches, eventually became a dead religion. In the seventeenth century, the Lord raised up a group of saints as a reaction to the deadness and emptiness of the reformed churches. These mystics, such as Madame Guyon, Father Fenelon, and Brother Lawrence, were used by the Lord to recover the experiences of the inner life. These saints, who still remained with the Roman Catholic Church, began to realize that life is God Himself in His Son by His Spirit. Although these saints knew something concerning Christ as the inner life, there was no practical church life with them. They were still in the sphere of the Roman Catholic Church. Many seekers of the Lord have been helped by Madame Guyon's autobiography. However, even though she had so much experience of the inner life, she still went to the statue of Mary. Although she was used by God as a reaction to the deadness of Protestantism, she was not clear about the church and she was not even clear about the idolatry in Catholicism.

THE FORMATION OF
PRIVATE CHURCHES AND FREE GROUPS

Throughout the history of the church, many groups of so-called puritans were raised up. These puritan groups were formed by leaders who saw something concerning the truth. Some saw that the proper baptism was by immersion. Spontaneously this was the beginning of the Baptist church. The Baptist denomination is one among many private churches, which may be considered as the fourth category of so-called church, in addition to the Roman Catholic Church, the Greek Orthodox Church, and the state churches. These private churches include the Baptist church, the Presbyterian church, the Methodist church, etc. Today there are many private churches. The fifth category of so-called church is the free groups. These free groups include all of the Bible churches. The Bible churches do not belong to the Roman Catholic Church, the Greek Orthodox Church, the state churches, or to any private denominations. Those in the Bible churches endeavor to have all their practices based on the Bible. In addition to these Bible churches, there are many other free groups which meet outside the denominations.

THE RECOVERY OF THE INITIAL STAGE OF THE CHURCH LIFE IN THE UNITY OF THE HOLY SPIRIT WITH ZINZENDORF AND THE MORAVIAN BRETHREN

History shows us that there was a desire within many seeking ones for the proper church life. They could not express this inward desire, but actually there was something in them seeking or hunting the proper church life. In the eighteenth century, the Lord moved among the Moravian brethren under the leadership of Count Zinzendorf to recover something of the practice of the church life. These Moravian brethren suffered the persecution not only of the Roman Catholic Church but also of the state churches. They were persecuted because they stood for the truth, and they fled to Zinzendorf's estate in Saxony for refuge. Because of Count Zinzendorf's love for the Lord, he received many of these seekers who came from different backgrounds. These brothers began to disagree over their doctrinal differences. One day Zinzendorf called a conference, and he convinced them to drop their doctrinal disagreements. They signed an agreement to keep the unity among them and to lay aside their differences in doctrine and in their religious backgrounds. Afterwards, while they were having the Lord's table, they experienced the outpouring of the Holy Spirit. Among them there was the strongest revival in church history up to that time, and they became one of the most prevailing Christian groups on earth. Even John Wesley was saved through them. He stayed with these brethren for a period of time. He said that if it were not for his burden for England, he would have stayed with the Moravian brethren for his entire life. To our knowledge, since the time of the early apostles, the Moravian brothers might be considered as the first group of Christians to realize the church life in a somewhat proper way. Therefore, God's blessing was poured out upon them. Although they enjoyed the practice of the church life to a certain degree, they were still not clear about many aspects of the truth concerning the church.

THE RECOVERED CHURCH LIFE WITH THE BRETHREN

In the nineteenth century, from 1825 to 1828, the Lord raised up the so-called Brethren under the leadership of John Nelson Darby. D. M. Panton said that the movement of the Brethren and its significance was far greater than the Reformation. The Reformation was somewhat worldly because of its association with human government, but the move among the Brethren was really something spiritual. They did not like to have any advertisements in their work for the Lord. It is even difficult for one to find a picture of J. N. Darby. Many of the Brethren felt that taking pictures was a worldly practice. Regretfully, the golden time of the Brethren lasted for only a short period of time. Eventually, there was a split among them. The first division was between J. N. Darby and Benjamin Newton. Their dispute was concerning the rapture of the believers. Darby was strong concerning pre-tribulation rapture, whereas Newton was strong concerning post-tribulation rapture.

Later, there was a second split among them. This division was between the so-called closed Brethren and the open Brethren. George Müller was one of the leading brothers among the Brethren. He was a real man of God. He was called the king of faith in the nineteenth century. He was so much with the Lord, but there was a big discrepancy between his understanding and Darby's realization. Darby and his followers insisted on not accepting any Christian who was still joined to a denomination. They considered all denominations as sin, evil. Thus, in their eyes, regardless of how good or spiritual a person was, as long as he remained in a denomination, he was considered by them as a companion of this evil. They considered a Christian in a denomination as an evil companion, and they would not receive him. George Müller, however, said that this was not fair. He said that many dear saints who were involved with the denominations were still very close to the Lord. He maintained that these believers could not be rejected and that they had to be received. This was the discrepancy between Darby and Müller, which led to another division among the Brethren. Thus, by this time there were three main groups among the Brethren—Benjamin Newton's group, the closed Brethren, and the open Brethren. The so-called Plymouth Brethren in this country mainly refers to the open Brethren. Within ninety years after the formation of the Brethren in 1828, they were divided into over one hundred divisions. Today there are all kinds of divisions among the Brethren. I was told by one sister among them that one group of Brethren was divided over whether or not to have an organ in their meetings.

Saints throughout the church's history have had different kinds of concepts concerning the rapture. Some believed in pre-tribulation rapture, others believed in post-tribulation rapture, and still others believed in a partial rapture, which takes place before and after the great tribulation. Forty years ago, I spent much time to study which school was the most scriptural. At that time Brother Nee gave us a number of messages on the truth concerning the rapture. He gave us a list of well-known believers who were found in all three schools of truth concerning the rapture. J. N. Darby, William Kelly, R. A. Torrey, Phillips Brooks, James Gray, Arno C. Gaebelein, J. A. Seiss, D. L. Moody, and C. I. Scofield are some of those who believed in pre-tribulation rapture. George Müller, A. J. Gordon, A. B. Simpson, W. J. Erdman, W. G. Moorehead, Henry Frost, James Wright, and Benjamin Newton believed in post-tribulation rapture. Hudson Taylor, Robert Chapman, Robert Govett, D. M. Panton, G. H. Pember, and Paul Rader believed in the rapture of the overcomers, which is called the partial rapture, or the mid-tribulation rapture. Paul Rader was the successor of R. A. Torrey in the Moody Memorial Church of Chicago. The doctrinal differences among the saints concerning the truth of the rapture caused much division.

Although the beginning of the divisions among the Brethren started over a disagreement concerning the rapture, the truths that were revealed to them greatly benefited all of the Lord's children. I would say that over ninety percent of the theology of fundamental Christianity came from the teaching of the Brethren. In the United States, many fundamental seminaries use the teachings of C. I. Scofield. Dr. Scofield was a great scholar and a student of the Brethren. Nearly ninety percent of what he wrote in his reference Bible and his Bible correspondence course was adopted from Brethren teaching. D. L. Moody said that if all the books in the entire world were to be burned, he would be satisfied to have a copy of the Bible and a copy of C. H. Mackintosh's notes on the Pentateuch. C. H. Mackintosh was a great teacher among the Brethren. Regardless of whether the fundamental denominations agreed with the Brethren move or not, their fundamental teaching was very much influenced by the Brethren teaching. In a sense, the Brethren teaching helped the so-called church, but in another sense, these teachings issued in divisions. The move among the Brethren at the beginning was really marvelous. This was a golden time that was a great help to the church life. Many spiritual, seeking Christians agree that this may have been the beginning of the fulfillment of the prophecy in the Lord's epistle to the church in Philadelphia in Revelation 3. However, due to the Brethren's overemphasis on doctrines, they were divided again and again.

THE LORD STARTING SOMETHING NEW ON VIRGIN SOIL

One hundred years after the beginning of the Brethren movement, the Lord started something new in mainland China. In the eighteenth century, the Moravian brethren were on the continent of Europe. In the nineteenth century, the Brethren were used by the Lord in England. A century later, the Lord moved in the Far East. I entered into the work with Brother Watchman Nee in Shanghai in 1933. I went to Brother Nee at least three or four times a week. He shared much with me concerning the history of the church. He told me that the Lord went to China to start something new. He said that the Lord was forced to come to China at the beginning of the twentieth century because in both Europe and America the field, soil, had been fully spoiled as far as the proper church life was concerned. Brother Nee spoke with me mostly in Chinese, but sometimes we used English terms. When he was speaking with me about the Lord's move in China, he used the English term *virgin soil*. I can never forget this term. He said that for the church life China was virgin soil at that time. Of course, this was the Lord's doing. One could never imagine that in such a heathen country full of the teachings of Confucius and the religion of Buddhism, the Lord would raise up something.

The first meeting in the Lord's recovery in China was in 1922 with Brother Nee in his hometown of Foochow. I am full of thanks to the Lord that in the first part of this century He gave Brother Nee as a gift to the Body. I was born in Christianity and raised up there. I even received my education in Christianity. In my seeking of the Lord, I passed through organized Christianity, fundamental Christianity, Brethren Christianity, and even Pentecostal Christianity. I also entered into the teachings of the inner-life Christians. In my entire life, I have never met a Christian who can compare with Brother Nee. I received the greatest and the highest help from him. He picked up good and helpful things from nearly every denomination, from every kind of Christian practice, and from all the seeking saints throughout the history of the church, and he passed them on to us. The first time I stayed with him I realized that he was standing on the shoulders of many who had gone before him.

Even before 1930 he had collected more than three thousand classical Christian books which contained Christian writings from the first century on. When he was between twenty and twenty-five years of age, his bedroom was full of books. There was only a narrow space for him to lie down between the rows of books. Sometimes we would say that Brother Nee was buried with books. I mainly came to know the history of the church, not from reading about it, but from Brother Nee's speaking with me. He related to me all the important things of church history. When he read something, there was no need for him to go back and review it. He could just relate to you what he read in a thorough and accurate way. He was a person who knew the Bible, who knew life, who knew the Lord, who knew the church, and who knew the history of the church. We received the greatest help from him, not in a narrow, sectarian way, but in an all-inclusive way.

When people came into our midst in the early days of the church life in China, they would wonder whether we were a Baptist church, a Presbyterian church, a Pentecostal church, or a Brethren church. This was because all the good aspects of the truth in these groups were among us. We baptized people as the Baptists did. We had the church government as the Presbyterians did. We experienced the outpouring of the Spirit, which the Pentecostals stressed. We also had the truths that the Brethren had released. We collected many good things that the Lord had recovered through all the saints, and we put them together in our church life.

BROTHER NEE'S SALVATION AND CALLING

Now I would like to begin relating the history of the local churches, beginning in the early 1920s in China. China was a country with an ancient culture, full of the teachings of Confucius and full of Buddhism. Eventually, however, the Lord sent His gospel there. The Lord's name, which is the Lord Himself, the Bible, and the gospel were brought to China. I believe that the Chinese version of the Bible is one of the better translations. We thank the Lord for this.

In 1920 there was a prevailing evangelist in China by the name of Dora Yu. She was saved when she was young and was sent by her family to England to study medicine. When her ship reached Marseilles, France, she went to the captain and told him that she had to go back to China to preach Christ. Thus, the captain sent her back. Her parents were extremely disappointed with her. Obviously, she came from a wealthy family who could send her to England to study medicine. But she was strong in her desire to preach Christ, and her family could not persuade her to do otherwise. They told her that they would have nothing to do with her and that she should go her way to preach her Jesus. From that time onward, she became prevailing in the preaching of the gospel.

In 1920 she was invited to Brother Nee's hometown, Foochow, which is close to the province of Kwantung, near Hong Kong. She was preaching the gospel in the Methodist church where Brother Nee's parents attended. Neither he nor his parents were saved at that time. Brother Nee's mother spoke English well, and his father had a good position in the Chinese customs. His mother was saved in one of these meetings with Dora Yu. Before being saved, his mother was very fond of playing mah-jong, a game of chance played by many of the Chinese. She was a very strong, talkative woman and was very dominant in their family, even over her husband. Brother Nee's father was a very nice gentleman who was very quiet. Brother Nee's family was composed of four brothers and four sisters, Brother Nee being the third child. The two children above him were sisters. The children also had the impression that their mother was too domineering at home. However, after their mother was saved in that gospel meeting, she came home and made a thorough confession to the whole family. She confessed all her failures and mistakes in a serious way. This was really the Lord's doing. Brother Nee was amazed that she could be converted like this through one meeting. He was so impressed by his mother's confession that he wanted to go and see what was there.

The next evening he went to listen to Dora Yu, and he was caught by the Lord. In those meetings many people wept with repentance. These meetings were very prevailing, and Brother Nee was fully caught. He was saved in the evening. That night, according to his testimony, he saw the Lord Jesus on the cross, and through that he was called by the Lord (see pp. 8-9 of *Watchman Nee's Testimony* published by Living Stream Ministry). He was called on the night he was saved. He told me this personally. He told me many things that he kept as a secret from others, and I realized that he was speaking to me for my training. After being called by the Lord, the Lord began to prepare him and use him in a marvelous way for His intention.

CHAPTER FOUR

THE HISTORY OF THE LOCAL CHURCHES

(2)

Scripture Reading: 1 Tim. 1:3-7, 19b-20; 4:1-3; 6:3-5, 20-21; 2 Tim. 1:15; 2:16-22; 3:5; 4:3-4, 14-15; Titus 1:10-11, 14; 3:10-11

In this chapter we want to continue our fellowship concerning the history of the Lord's recovery among us in the past fifty years. In the previous chapter, we shared how Brother Nee was saved and called in the same night. We have to remember that he was saved through a woman evangelist who was a native of China. The Lord raised up such a gift as Brother Nee through a native sister.

THE LORD'S PREPARATION OF BROTHER NEE
THROUGH SISTER M. E. BARBER

After Brother Nee's conversion, he came into contact with an older sister by the name of M. E. Barber. Miss Barber was about sixty years old when Brother Nee met her. She was from England. When she was young, around thirty years old, she was sent by a Methodist mission to Brother Nee's province in China. While she was there, her co-missionaries fabricated a case against her because of their jealousy of her. Because of these false reports, the mission board called her back.

She was a person who knew the Lord in a living way, and she was always exercising to learn the lessons of the cross. When she returned, she made a decision not to say a word in vindication of herself. She stayed in England for a number of years. At a certain point, the chairman of the mission board came to realize that she had been accused falsely. He asked her to tell him the truth. He said to Miss Barber, "I know you are learning the lessons of the cross and that you

would not say anything for yourself. Since you have learned
something of the Lord's authority, I am asking you as one of
your authorities to tell me the truth." Thus, Miss Barber took
this standing to tell the truth concerning her case. She was
vindicated, and the board immediately made the decision to
send her back.

Before that time, she began to know the way of the Lord
concerning His church. She came into contact with D. M.
Panton, who was a student of the great teacher Robert Govett.
Brother Panton came to know the evils of denominationalism,
and he met with a group of others outside of the denominations. In today's light, we can see that he was not so clear,
on the positive side, concerning the proper practice of the
proper church life, but he was very clear, on the negative
side, concerning denominationalism. After Miss Barber contacted D. M. Panton's group, she became clear about
denominations. Then she resigned from her post as a
missionary in the Methodist mission. After much prayer, she
became clear that the Lord would send her back to China
according to His leading and not through any mission. She
went back to China, in human terms, on her own. She went
back on her own to work for the Lord, and she selected a
very small town just outside of Brother Nee's hometown,
Foochow. The suburban town where she stayed was called
Pagoda. Miss Barber stayed there without traveling much
and without any advertisement. She just stayed there and
prayed day and night.

Brother Nee came into contact with her soon after his
conversion, and he received so much help from her. He spent
at least several times with me personally to tell me the things
concerning his relationship with Miss Barber. Initially,
Brother Nee was among a group of young brothers and sisters
who had just been saved and went to contact Miss Barber.
Miss Barber was deep and also very strict. In her strictness,
she used to rebuke the ones under her perfecting. Eventually,
the only one that still went to see Miss Barber after a period
of time was Brother Nee. Brother Nee told me that whenever
he went to her, he was always rebuked. He told me that the
more she rebuked him, the more he sent himself to her for

her rebuking. He said that he did this because he received the help from her.

In 1936 I was invited to the central part of China. After a few days, Brother Nee was also invited there, and we stayed together. He said to me, "Brother Lee, if Miss Barber were still living, we would be much better than what we are today." Then he said, "In 1933 I went to Europe to visit many spiritual persons. In my being, according to my weighing, no spiritual person whom I visited in the Western world at that time could compare spiritually with Miss Barber." This shows us the kind of preparation the Lord made for Brother Nee as His gift, His servant.

Miss Barber went to the Lord in 1929. That was nearly the same year in which Brother Nee finished his writing of *The Spiritual Man*. Miss Barber, in her will, gave all her things to Brother Nee. Of course, she did not have many personal things, but she willed Brother Nee her Bible with all her notes in it. That was very precious. Later, Brother Nee told me that he was thinking of writing a biography of M. E. Barber, but he could not find the time to do it. It was a real loss to us that Brother Nee never found the time to write such a biography. If he had been able to do this, it would have been a great help to us even today.

According to what Brother Nee told me, Sister Barber was a person who always lived in the presence of the Lord. One day Brother Nee went to see her. She was in another room while he was waiting in the living room. He told me that while he was waiting there, he had a deep sense of the Lord's presence there. She was a deep person in the Lord, and she composed a number of excellent hymns which are in our hymnal. All her hymns were very deep in the Lord.

Furthermore, day by day she was waiting for the Lord's coming back. On the last day of 1926, she was taking a walk with Brother Nee. When they turned the corner to another street she said to Brother Nee, "Maybe as we turn this corner, we will meet Him." She was a person waiting for the Lord's return. She lived and walked in the presence of our returning Lord. I never met her, but after I heard what Brother Nee told me, I received a great help.

It was through M. E. Barber that he received the foundation of his spiritual life. Brother Nee would tell people that it was through a sister that he got saved, and it was also through a sister that he was edified. As a British person from the Western world, Sister Barber came to know the famous spiritual giants in Christianity at her time. Through Sister Barber, Brother Nee came to know the top spiritual books by people such as Robert Govett, D. M. Panton, and Jesse Penn-Lewis. The best publications on the exposition of the Bible and church history were introduced to Brother Nee through her.

Brother Nee was a marvelous reader and an excellent discerner and selector of the things of Christ for the Christian life and the church life. He himself told me that in his early days of ministry he gave back one third of his income to the Lord, kept one third for his living, and spent the other third to buy books to read.

The first year that I went to Shanghai, I stayed with Brother Nee as his guest. One day he came upstairs to my living quarters with two bundles of books. He put them on my bed and said, "This is something for you," and he went away. He had given me Dean Alford's four-volume work entitled *The New Testament for English Readers*. Dean Alford was an authority on the Greek words of the New Testament. This four-volume set rendered me great help in knowing the Bible. The other books given to me by Brother Nee were John Nelson Darby's five-volume *Synopsis of the Books of the Bible*. His synopsis of the Scriptures can be considered as the best among all the expositions. I received great help from his synopsis.

Brother Nee told me that he had notified the book stores in London which carried secondhand books. Whenever they received something ordered by him, they would send it to him and he would pay the bill. In this way he collected all the major classical Christian writings from the first century to the present day. He had one of the best libraries on the history of the church, including the biographies and autobiographies of the spiritual giants throughout the centuries with their master writings.

For more details of Brother Nee's life, I would recommend *Watchman Nee's Testimony*, compiled by Brother K. H. Weigh. This book includes three messages of Brother Nee's own testimony, which he gave in 1936. They cover the first sixteen years of Brother Nee's spiritual life. Brother Weigh was a classmate of Brother Nee's, he was saved through Brother Nee, and he was also a co-worker with Brother Nee.

Now I will begin presenting the things of the past fifty years in a few categories. First, we want to see the revelations the Lord has given us in these past fifty years. Second, we want to see something concerning the practice of the church life. Third, we would like to see something concerning Brother Nee's work, including his traveling and his publications. Then we want to fellowship concerning the sufferings of Brother Nee—the attacks and the persecution he suffered throughout his ministry. I want to cover these main categories of the past history among us. In this chapter I would like to relate the revelations we have received from the Lord in these past fifty years up to 1973. I will enumerate forty-six major items.

REVELATIONS RECEIVED FROM THE LORD (1922-1973)

1. The Assurance of Salvation

The first thing the Lord showed us through Brother Nee was the assurance of salvation. The Lord sent many men of God to China as missionaries. They preached the gospel, but they did not help people to know that they were saved. Before Brother Nee was raised up, no one had made the assurance of salvation clear among the Chinese. Although they knew they were Christians, they did not think that a person could know he was saved. They thought that it was too proud for a person to say that he knew he was saved. Their concept was that they believed in the Lord Jesus, and they would do their best until the day they would see Him. In that day they would know whether or not they were saved. To them it was only at that time they would be assured of their salvation. They did not believe you could have the assurance of salvation today.

Many of the Chinese were really saved. In a sense, they realized that they were children of God, but if you checked with them, they would not say that they were saved. Then the Lord raised up Brother Nee. He was so clear about the assurance of salvation, and this was the first thing which he saw from the Lord and ministered to the believers. Even by the time I entered into the work with him in 1933, we were still speaking messages on the assurance of salvation. We always helped people to hold on to one verse for their assurance. This is because their assurance was in the written Word of God with the inspiration of the Holy Spirit. We would ask people to read a verse like John 3:16 until they realized that they were assured of their salvation.

2. The Deviation of Christianity

After Brother Nee was saved, he made the decision to read the entire Bible. Through his reading of the Bible, the Lord showed him the deviation of Christianity. Christianity had deviated from the Scriptures and from the Lord's way. Much of the practice of today's Christianity is a deviation from the holy Word.

3. The Church

Mainly through Brother Nee, the Lord showed us the church. This is the third main revelation the Lord gave us. We saw the church as the Body of Christ. Brother Nee told people that the church is not a building, an organization of Christianity, or a mission. He declared that the church is an organism, the Body of Christ, and that in another sense, the church is the *ekklesia*, a Greek word referring to the church as the called-out assembly.

4. The Denominations

The Lord also showed us the evils, the wrongdoings, of denominationalism. Christians have denominated themselves with many different names such as Lutheran, Wesleyan, Anglican, Presbyterian, Baptist, etc. These denominations are divisions.

5. The Clergy-laity System

The Lord showed us how the clergy-laity system kills the functioning of the members of the Body of Christ. This system includes human organization with its hierarchy, rank, and position. In the Roman Catholic Church, there are the priests, the bishops, the archbishops, the cardinals, and the pope. In the Protestant churches, there are the pastors, and in the state churches there are the bishops and the heads of state. According to the revelation of the Scriptures, this system is an evil abomination in the eyes of God. Denominationalism cuts the Body into pieces, and the clergy-laity system kills the functions of the members of the Body. By these two things, the entire Body of Christ is brought to nothing.

6. The Universal Priesthood

We spent much time to teach the believers that all of them were priests and that they could function in a priestly service to the Lord.

7. The Presbytery

The church does not need any organization or any kind of human government or rule, but the church does need a proper presbytery. The presbytery is the eldership. Every local church needs a group of experienced brothers to be the leading ones, the overseers, taking the oversight of the church's activity.

8. The Proper Baptism and the Proper Lord's Table

The Lord showed us the proper baptism, which is by being immersed into water. He also showed us the proper way to have His table.

9. Head Covering and the Laying On of Hands

The Lord showed Brother Nee the real meaning of head covering and the real practice of laying hands on the saints.

10. Living by Faith in God

We learned to serve the Lord in the way of not being hired

by anyone, that is, by any mission, organization, or so-called church. We learned to live by faith in God. Watchman Nee took the lead among us to live in this way. In *Watchman Nee's Testimony*, Brother Nee shares his experience of living a life of faith (pp. 44-55).

11. Divine Healing

Through Brother Nee's experience, we were brought into a realization of the proper divine healing that builds up the inner life. The divine healing which Brother Nee saw and experienced was not just an outward gift, but a healing that resulted in inward building up. Brother Nee himself experienced such a healing. He was close to death with tuberculosis in 1929. He was so ill that he could not even rise up from bed to walk. One day he received a particular word from God in the Scriptures. He stood on that word and rose up from bed. He walked to a saint's home where some brothers and sisters had gathered together to pray for him. When he spoke to them of his healing, they all were full of thanksgiving and praise (see *Watchman Nee's Testimony*, pp. 30-38).

12. The Death, the Resurrection, the Ascension, and the Second Coming of Christ

The Lord showed Brother Nee so much concerning the all-inclusive death of Christ in both its objective and subjective aspects. He also showed Brother Nee much truth concerning the resurrection, the ascension, and the second coming of Christ. In 1925 I began to read some of his publications on these truths.

13. The Indwelling of the Holy Spirit

The crucified, resurrected, ascended, and coming Christ is now indwelling our spirit by His Spirit. Brother Nee spent much time on the truth concerning the indwelling Spirit.

14. The Outpouring of the Holy Spirit

Brother Nee himself had a rich experience of the outpoured Holy Spirit, but he never spoke in tongues. He referred to the baptism of the Holy Spirit as the outpouring of the Holy Spirit.

15. The Tripartite Man

Sometime before 1925 Brother Nee saw man's three parts. Later, he wrote *The Spiritual Man*. Among all the Chinese writings of Christians, I do not believe that there has ever been a book written with such a clear vision concerning the spirit, soul, and body of man. The main point of the truth concerning the tripartite man is the human spirit.

16. Sanctification by Faith

Also before 1925 Brother Nee saw the truth concerning sanctification by faith. He pointed out that John Wesley's teaching of holiness was actually not holiness but the desire for sinless perfection, human perfection without any sin. He also pointed out what the Brethren had seen. They pointed out what the Lord said in Matthew 23 concerning the temple sanctifying the gold and the altar sanctifying the gift. The common gold was made holy positionally by changing its position from a common place to a holy one (v. 17). When the gold was in the temple, it was sanctified. The Lord also pointed out that the altar sanctifies the gift (v. 19). The common animals offered on the altar were sanctified. This is a positional sanctification by changing the gift's location from a common place to a holy one. The Brethren also pointed out that the food we eat is sanctified through prayer. This is according to 1 Timothy 4:4-5. The Brethren saw the truth concerning positional sanctification.

Brother Nee went on to show us that sanctification is not only positional but also dispositional. The dispositional change that takes place from sanctification is transformation. In His dispositional sanctification the Lord saturates us with Himself, adding Himself as the new element into our being to transform us into His image.

17. The Inner Life

Through Brother Nee's ministry, we were brought into the vision and experience of the inner life in a rich way. The mystics in the seventeenth century saw something concerning the inner life, but they did not see as much as the Lord has shown us today.

18. The Overcomers

Because of the church's degradation, many Christians have been defeated. Thus, the Lord calls some to be the overcomers. This truth is seen in the seven epistles to the seven churches in Revelation 2 and 3. In the degradation of the church, the Lord sounds out His call for some of His lovers to be overcomers.

19. The Kingdom

Along with the revelation concerning the overcomers, Brother Nee saw the truth concerning the kingdom. He was mainly helped by the teachings of Govett and Panton. The truth concerning the kingdom is scriptural and deep. Much of fundamental, traditional theology condemns the revelation of the kingdom truths. According to the proper teaching of the New Testament, not all the believers will enter into the kingdom of the heavens, the thousand-year kingdom, when the Lord returns. Only the overcomers will be kings with Him in the millennium. The kingship with the Lord Jesus in the coming age will be a reward to the overcoming saints.

20. The Rapture

The revelation of the rapture goes along with the revelation of the kingdom. In the general teaching of today's fundamental theology, people are told that the entire church will be raptured before the tribulation. However, according to the truth of the Scripture, this is altogether wrong. As we pointed out in the previous chapter, Brother Nee saw that there was a difference among the saints concerning their belief concerning the rapture. According to the truth, the overcomers will be raptured before the tribulation.

The kingdom is a matter of reward, and rapture is a matter of maturity. To be raptured can be compared to a crop being harvested from the field. The crop cannot be harvested when it is not ripe. When the crop is ripe with the maturity

in life, the farmer takes it from the field and puts it into the
barn. Thus, all of us need to become ripe in life. We need
the maturity. Then the Lord will harvest us. Brother Nee
saw the revelation concerning the overcomers and the
kingdom as a reward to the overcomers. He also saw the
truth concerning the rapture, which needs the maturity of
the saints.

21. Spiritual Warfare

Somewhere around 1925, Brother Nee began to see the
truth concerning spiritual warfare. He saw God's divine
purpose and that there is the need of spiritual warfare for
the accomplishment of God's divine purpose in this universe.
Especially on this earth, there is a conflict, a war, between
God and His enemy, Satan. This warfare involves all of God's
children. If we take sides with Satan, we are fighting against
God. If we take sides with God, we are fighting against Satan.
All the overcoming saints have to realize that they are on
the battlefield fighting for God's divine purpose. Brother Nee
called a conference in 1928 in Shanghai and gave a number
of messages concerning spiritual warfare.

22. The Centrality and Universality of Christ

Brother Nee called a conference in Shanghai in January
of 1934 to speak concerning the centrality and universality
of Christ. I was responsible for publishing these messages in
Chinese. These were marvelous messages showing us that
Christ is the center and the circumference of the entire
universe for God's eternal purpose.

23. The Boundary of a Local Church

Brother Nee saw the truth concerning the boundary of a
local church in 1933 and 1934. In 1933 he was invited by
the Brethren to visit them in England. They also took him
to Canada and the United States. At that time he saw the
confusion and the division among the Brethren assemblies.
In one city there could be several Brethren assemblies. This
troubled Brother Nee, so he spent one year to read and study
the New Testament again to find out what the boundary of

a local assembly, a local church, was. Eventually, he saw that the New Testament reveals clearly that the boundary of a local church is the boundary of the locality (city) in which the local church stands. In January of 1934, he gave four main messages on this truth, and these were published in the same year in a book entitled *The Meeting Life*. Brother Nee asked me to write the foreword for this book.

24. The Overcoming Life

By 1934 many believers had given up the denominations to turn the way of the Lord's recovery in China, but most of them paid too much attention to external things, such as the leaving of the denominations, head covering, baptism, etc. Because of this, Brother Nee was very burdened. He had seen the truth concerning the overcoming life, but in 1935 he saw it in a more prevailing way. In August of 1935 he held a conference with us on the overcoming life of Christ. He stayed with me as my guest in my hometown for this conference. This conference brought in a prevailing revival among us, starting from my hometown in northern China. He also shared these messages when he returned to Shanghai in 1935.

25. The Ground of a Local Church

At the beginning of 1937, Brother Nee began to see not only the boundary of a local church but also the ground of a local church. Because of the confusion in Christianity, Brother Nee went back to the New Testament to research the truth concerning the practical expression of the church. According to his study and research of the New Testament, he found out that one city should have only one church. A local church is a church in a city. The ground of a local church is the ground of unity, which also may be called the ground of locality. If we are in Los Angeles, we should meet as the church in Los Angeles. If we are in San Diego, we should meet as the church in San Diego. This is not only scriptural but also logical.

Brother Nee gave the messages concerning the ground of locality in 1937. I and other workers were working in

Tientsin, the biggest port in northern China, when we received a cable from Brother Nee in Shanghai asking us to come on New Year's Day for an urgent conference with him. At that time he gave the messages that are now contained in the book *The Normal Christian Church Life*. The Chinese edition was entitled *Rethinking Our Missions,* and the English edition was entitled *Concerning Our Missions*. During this conference in January of 1937, Brother Nee became sick. Therefore, he repeated the messages in September and October of that year after the Japanese army had invaded China. Many of us retreated to the interior of China, and we assembled at Hankow where Brother Nee gave all the messages again to a greater number. At this point we became so clear about the church within and without. We became clear about the contents of the church and the practice of the church.

26. The Practicality of the Church Life

After seeing the ground of the church, Brother Nee became clear concerning the practicality of the church life. I still remember the day in 1940 when I was in Shanghai attending his training. On this day he and I were walking down a staircase. He showed me his hand and said, "Brother, we have the blueprint in our hand concerning the church life." After he said this, I wondered what the blueprint was. I wanted to see this blueprint. Praise the Lord! Eventually, Brother Nee showed us the blueprint of the practicality of the church life.

We should not think that our present practice of the church life is a light thing. In Shanghai in 1940 I saw the blueprint of the practicality of the church life, and I brought it to northern China to put it into practice. I have to testify that it really works. Through the outworking of this blueprint, a big revival was brought to northern China. We enjoyed such a revival through the practice of the church life according to the blueprint Brother Nee had received from the Lord.

27. The Body of Christ

From 1940 Brother Nee always stressed the Body of

Christ. He was very burdened that we would see the Body. He gave message after message and conference after conference, always stressing this one thing—seeing the Body. Brother Nee was very nice, gentle, and kind, but with us trainees, he was very frank at times. He would ask if we had seen the Body, and then he would ask some to give a testimony of what they had supposedly seen. After their testimony he would say, "You haven't seen the Body." Then he would point out what they said to prove that they had not seen the Body and that the Body was merely a theory or a doctrine to them. We may know the Body doctrinally, but it may not be real to us. He stressed again and again that we need the vision of the Body.

28. The Authority of the Church

Brother Nee also stressed the authority of the church. He imparted this vision to the church from 1940 through 1942.

29. Coordination

Along with the vision of the Body of Christ, and the truth concerning the authority of the church, Brother Nee shared concerning coordination for the practicality of the church life. Our practical life in the church should be in coordination with the members of the Body.

30. The Preaching of the Gospel by the Church

Beginning in 1940 we began to see the preaching of the gospel by the church. This preaching is not merely by some individual evangelist, but by the entire church. The result of such evangelism by the church was very fruitful.

31. Migration

In 1942 and 1943 the church in the Lord's recovery began to see the need for migration. The first migration among us was from northern China to Inner Mongolia. Seventy adults with all their children migrated from my hometown to a city in Inner Mongolia. They all made this trip in one boat. At another time thirty adults from my hometown migrated to a town in the southern part of Manchuria. The migrating of the saints spread the church life to other parts of the country.

32. The Church Being Local and the Work Being Regional

After the war in 1948, Brother Nee began to see that the church is local, but the work is regional. The church is a matter of locality, but the work is a matter of a region, a district. This truth is covered in the last chapter of *Further Talks on the Church Life.*

33. The Breaking of the Outer Man and the Release of the Spirit

In all the suffering through which Brother Nee passed, he learned one basic lesson—the breaking of the outer man and the release of the spirit. There is a book published called *The Release of the Spirit* which contains Brother Nee's sharing on this truth. Actually, the title of this book is not so appropriate. What Brother Nee shared is more on the breaking of the outer man, whereas the release of the spirit is an issue, an outcome, of the breaking of the outer man.

In 1946 I was in Shanghai, and I stayed there close to three years. Whenever I was with Brother Nee, he always stressed that there was the need of the breaking of our natural man. Our outer man, our self, our natural makeup, has to be broken. All the things which happen to us are governed by the Holy Spirit to discipline us, and this is for the breaking of our natural man so that our spirit, in which the Holy Spirit dwells, may be released. When our spirit is released, the Holy Spirit is spontaneously released with our spirit.

Brother Nee told us that whenever we give a message, we need to give it with the release of our spirit. However, he went on to say that it is not so easy to have our spirit released as long as we are still living in the natural life. The natural man is like a shell containing our spirit. Therefore, we need the breaking of the outer shell, so that the inner spirit can be released. Then the Spirit of God with Christ will be richly ministered to others. This is the truth

concerning the breaking of the outer man and the release of
the spirit.

I am not so happy about some of the translations of
Brother Nee's books, because they do not convey the exact
meaning which Brother Nee wanted to convey. He explained
to me his burden concerning the breaking of the outer man
and the release of the spirit even before he gave messages
on this subject. I am concerned that many readers of the
book entitled *The Release of the Spirit* would think that the
release of the spirit is the release of the Holy Spirit. This is
not according to the truth. The release of the spirit is not
the release of the Holy Spirit, but the release of our spirit.
When our spirit is released, the Holy Spirit is also released
with our spirit. In order to have this accomplished, our
natural man, the outer man, has to be broken.

34. Knowing and Exercising the Human Spirit

Even before 1924 Brother Nee saw the tripartite man.
Later we had to be helped to know the human spirit and to
exercise, to use, the human spirit. We were taught to turn
to our spirit and to stay in our spirit. Our human spirit can
be likened to an electrical switch. In order to apply the
electricity in a building, we have to turn on the switch. Our
spirit is the switch to apply all the things of Christ as the
Spirit.

35. The Actual Building Up

Brother Nee stressed that we all need an actual building
up in the Body of Christ. We should not just have a doctrinal
talk about the building. Brother Nee said that we had to
consider who we have actually been built up with. He said,
"You may be a good speaker who can give many messages
on building up, but with whom have you ever been built up?"
We need the actual building up. After the war, every time
Brother Nee spoke, he was always either on the breaking of
the outer man or on the building up. When Brother Nee
asked us who we were built up with, this put us all on the
spot. Not many could give an adequate answer because we
were all exposed. Although Brother Nee was very nice and

gentle, he was also very frank and strict with his trainees. Sometimes he adjusted me in a bold way, and I received much help from his training.

36. Christ, the Life-giving Spirit

Christ today is the life-giving Spirit. First Corinthians 15:45b tells us that the last Adam, Christ, became a life-giving Spirit. I cannot tell you how much life this one point has brought to the church!

37. Enjoying the Lord— Eating and Drinking the Lord

After 1948, we began to see how to eat and drink the Lord. In other words, we began to see that we need to enjoy the Lord. This also includes the revelation of Christ as the tree of life, good for food.

38. Pray-reading

In 1966 we were brought into the practice of pray-reading the Word of God.

39. Calling on the Lord

In 1967 we saw the truth concerning calling on the name of the Lord.

40. Breathing the Lord

We also saw that we need to breathe in the Lord as the holy *pneuma*, the holy breath, the Holy Spirit.

41. The Universal Prophesying

In 1968 we saw that everyone has to prophesy. We can all prophesy one by one (1 Cor. 14:31).

42. The Sevenfold Intensified Spirit

The Lord showed us the sevenfold intensified Spirit in 1969 in Erie, Pennsylvania.

43. Christ versus Religion

In 1970 we saw the revelation of Christ versus religion in an international conference in Los Angeles, California.

44. The Church as the New Man

The Lord showed us clearly in 1970 that the church is not only the Body of Christ but also the new man.

45. Christ as the Person of the Church

In 1971 we saw the truth concerning Christ as our person.

46. The Abolishing of the Ordinances

Later we saw the truth concerning Christ's abolishing all the ordinances on the cross.

CHRIST AND THE CHURCH

The totality of the items listed above is Christ and the church, the great mystery. Christ is the content, and the church is the expression. In other words, Christ is our life within, and the church is our living without. The church is our daily living.

(Editor's note: A list of ten major items recovered from 1958 to 1989 can be found in *The Present Advance of the Lord's Recovery*, pp. 8-9.)

CHAPTER FIVE

THE HISTORY OF THE LOCAL CHURCHES

(3)

Scripture Reading: 2 Pet. 1:2, 15; 3:3-4; 1 John 2:18-19, 22; 4:1-3; 2 John 7, 9-11; 3 John 9-10; Jude 3-4, 11-13, 17-21

I would like to say again that I hope we would pray-read the verses in the Scripture reading. When we pray them into us, we will be able to see the proper church life with Christ as our life.

THE PRACTICE OF THE CHURCH LIFE

In the previous chapter, we saw the main revelations which the Lord has shown us in the past fifty years. In this chapter we want to see the practice of the church life in the Lord's recovery throughout the past fifty years.

The Beginning of the Church Life in Brother Nee's Hometown

The practice of the church life among us started in 1922, two years after Brother Nee was saved. The first local church was established in his hometown, Foochow, in southern China. He and some other young Christians saw that Christianity had deviated from God's way as revealed in the Bible. Not more than ten of them began to meet in a sister's home, but after two years, something very negative happened. The husband of this sister became a popular evangelist among the Chinese Christians. He met a missionary of the Christian and Missionary Alliance in Shanghai named Mr. Woodbury. Mr. Woodbury was a man of God, but he was in the denominations. He advised this brother to be formally or-dained so that he could be invited by all the so-called Christian churches. An appointment was made for Mr. Woodbury to come from Shanghai to Foochow to ordain this brother.

When Brother Nee found out about this, he gave a message in one of the meetings on the history of the ark in the Old Testament. The tabernacle with the ark was built according to God's heavenly design. The tabernacle typifies the church, and the ark typifies Christ. When the children of Israel were in a normal situation, the ark was in the tabernacle. When they became abnormal, the ark was captured away. In that abnormal time, the ark was in one place, and the empty tabernacle was in another place. Brother Nee was only twenty-one years old, but he could give such a message on the history of the ark, pointing out that we Christians today are in an abnormal situation. In the abnormal situation, God does not care for the empty tabernacle but for the ark, Christ. Brother Nee applied this by saying that God does not care for outward things such as being formally ordained to be a so-called minister. Notes were taken of Brother Nee's message, and I was able to read them nine years later. This message was very revealing.

Because of this message, Brother Nee was excommunicated by six brothers. The leading one was this brother who was the evangelist, Leland Wang. Brother Nee related this entire story to me in 1933. It took him hours to tell me the whole story. Because of his excommunication, the meeting in Foochow became a "marsh" (cf. Ezek. 47:11). Brother Nee referred to this as a halfway shelter in some of his writings. He likened such a meeting to some of the people of Israel coming out of captivity in Babylon but never returning and entering into Jerusalem, staying halfway between Babylon and Jerusalem. Over ninety percent of the people who met in Foochow were converted through Brother Nee's preaching. Many of them came to Brother Nee and told him they did not agree that he would be put out of the church. He told them, however, that he felt deeply that he had to learn the lesson of the cross, so he decided to leave.

The Spreading of the Church Life

Brother Nee then left Foochow and went to a place called Pagoda. In 1925 he began to publish a magazine called *The Christian*. At the end of 1926, he was led by the Lord to go to Shanghai and Nanking, the capital of China at that time, to start a work. The church was raised up in Shanghai at the end of 1926 and the early part of 1927. Eventually, the church in Shanghai became the biggest church, the leading church, and the central church in China. From Shanghai the church practice spread throughout China. In 1932 the practice of the church life spread to the north, beginning in Chefoo, my hometown. It spread to Tientsin, the biggest seaport in the north, and to Peking. In 1933 the church practice also spread to Manchuria, the place where Japan began its war against China. In 1934 the church life continued to spread to many places in China proper from Shanghai and from Chefoo. In 1937 many of the Chinese retreated to western China due to the Japanese invasion. Many brothers also went to the west to begin the church life. The church life began in 1937 in Chungking, the capital of China during the war. From 1938 to 1939 the church life spread to Hong Kong. In 1943 the church life migrated to Inner Mongolia from my hometown. Within about one year, over forty local churches were raised up in Inner Mongolia through seventy who migrated there from Chefoo. In 1948 and 1949 after the war, there was a great revival among us. Through that revival the church life spread into most of the cities. By 1949 there were hundreds of local churches in China. There were local churches in each of its thirty-three provinces and in all the leading cities.

It was also in 1949 that the Communists took over mainland China. About three hundred fifty to five hundred saints among us went to the island of Taiwan from mainland China. Some went there in 1947 to begin the church life with a very small number. In 1948 the number was strengthened. In 1949 I was also sent by the work to Taiwan. Within the next six years, our number grew from about five hundred to about twenty thousand. Now on the island of Taiwan there are about seventy local churches. The church in Taipei today has over twenty-one thousand saints meeting in fourteen halls (editor's note—this was in 1973).

The Lord also moved in Southeast Asia through Brother Nee. In 1924 at the age of twenty-one, he went to Malaysia.

That was the year he was excommunicated from the meeting in Foochow. He went to a city called Sitiawan to visit with his mother. Through that visit the first local church was raised up in Southeast Asia. From 1931 through 1933 the church life spread from China through the immigrating Chinese to places such as Singapore and other cities of Malaysia and Indonesia. Then in 1950 the proper church life went to the Philippines in Manila. In 1957 the church life spread to Japan. In 1958 the church life spread to the United States beginning in San Francisco. In 1959 the church life spread to Brazil, in 1963 to Canada, in 1965 to South Korea, in 1970 to New Zealand and Australia, in 1971 to Germany and Nigeria, and in 1972 to Ghana. These years and places will give us some view of the spreading of the church life on this earth.

A BRIEF SKETCH OF BROTHER NEE'S WORK

Preaching the Gospel to His Classmates

Now that we have seen the revelations the Lord has given us and the practice of the church life from our history, we want to see the work of Brother Nee. Immediately after being saved in 1920, Brother Nee began to work for the Lord. He was still a student in high school. After he was saved, he started to preach the gospel to his classmates. He told me personally that he fasted and prayed every Saturday in preparation for preaching the gospel to his classmates the next day. His school had less than one hundred fifty students. Within about one year, nearly all the students in the school were saved. Through his preaching there was a real revival in that school. By that time on the campus, one could see students sitting and reading the Bible under the trees and others studying the Bible and praying together on the lawn.

Early Publications

In 1922 the church life began in Brother Nee's hometown. In 1923 he published his first magazine called *The Present Testimony*. I read this early in 1925, and it was very hard for me to understand because it was so deep. I received a copy of this publication from my second sister, who was studying at a women's seminary in Nanking. She received one copy of Brother Nee's writings and brought it home in the summer. *The Present Testimony* contained articles concerning the principles of the death, resurrection, and ascension of Christ.

In 1924 Brother Nee was excommunicated from the meeting in his hometown. He moved to Pagoda, and in 1925 he began to publish his second magazine called *The Christian*. This was a monthly publication, usually of about sixty or seventy pages. In that paper Brother Nee expounded the first three chapters of Revelation, and he spent much time on the seven epistles to the seven churches in chapters two and three. Through those messages on the seven epistles, the fallen situation of Christianity was exposed, and the proper church life was revealed. Many young people throughout China read those messages, and their eyes were opened. I was one of those young people. Through those messages I saw the evils of denominationalism, and I also saw a vision of the church. This magazine had a total of twenty-four issues. Those who read these issues in a proper way received revelation and inspiration. It was amazing how Brother Nee could expound the Scriptures in such a marvelous way at the age of twenty-two. In this magazine he also expounded the first two chapters of Genesis. He applied all the days of God's creation to Christ. He shared that the land which appeared on the third day out of the waters was a picture of Christ coming out of death. Christ was the good land resurrected on the third day to produce all kinds of life.

The Beginning of the Church Life in Shanghai and Brother Nee's Contact with the Brethren

In 1926 Brother Nee went to Shanghai to begin the church life there. Between 1922 and 1927, Brother Nee was invited to minister in many places in Christianity, but after the church in Shanghai was raised up and became strong, he received only a few invitations. From 1927 until Brother Nee went into glory, he was invited only once by the denominations, and that was to a Southern Baptist seminary in my hometown. That was when we first met, and he stayed in my home. In 1938 and 1939 he was invited to England and Scandinavia by some Christians there. That invitation was in a different category.

During the years 1925 through 1927, Brother Nee read some of the writings of the British Brethren, the closed Brethren. As we have pointed out, the Brethren were raised up by the Lord around 1825 to 1828, but within about fifteen years, they were divided into three big divisions. One group was with Darby, which was considered as the exclusive Brethren, the closed Brethren. Another group under the leadership of George Müller was considered as the open Brethren, or Plymouth Brethren. The strictest group was under the leadership of Benjamin Newton, who disagreed with Darby concerning the rapture of the saints. Brother Nee read many of the writings of John Nelson Darby. These writings were marvelous, and he received much help from them. Due to the help Brother Nee received, the way we conducted our meetings in the early days of the church life was very close to the Brethren way. Some even called us the Chinese version of the British Brethren.

Brother Nee picked up all the good points from different kinds of Christian practices and put them together in the church life. The Brethren, especially in England, found out that there was a group of Christians who had been raised up by the Lord in a wonderful way, so they started to correspond with Brother Nee. Then they proposed that they would send some to visit us. Brother Nee agreed to receive them, but he told them not to bring in their background. They promised they would not do this, so they came to Shanghai in 1931. This group of closed Brethren was considered to be the best among the Brethren at that time. A brother by the name of James Taylor was their teacher. Elden Hall, which was the first hall of the church in Los Angeles, was originally their hall. We bought Elden Hall from James Taylor's son in 1965. Among the ones that came to Shanghai were Charles Barlow and W. J. House. These two were the speakers among them. Instead of coming to us as simple believers according to their agreement, they brought the so-called Brethren practice with them. This caused much trouble, and this was a hard situation for Brother Nee to handle.

They invited Brother Nee to visit them, and he did in 1933. He traveled through France and stayed in England for some time. A brother in England brought him to the United States and to Vancouver, Canada. James Taylor wrote many letters, and there is a record of his correspondence with Brother Nee during this time. In that same year Brother Nee returned to China from Europe. During that time I was fully brought into the work in Shanghai with him. He personally told me everything concerning his visit abroad. The Brethren promised him that if he would take their way, they would buy him some land to build a big hall in Shanghai. They also promised him other things. He said "no" to all their proposals.

Victory Conferences

Before his visit to the Brethren, Brother Nee had two conferences. He called these conferences "victory conferences." One was in 1928, and the other was in 1931 when the Brethren came to Shanghai. In 1934 he had the third victory conference. In that ten-day conference, he gave messages on the centrality and universality of Christ. I was in that entire conference. Brother Nee asked me to give a message on the Lord's Day to all the visitors as an introduction to the conference. I was also responsible for keeping a record of all these messages by longhand notes. I received a deep impression from this conference and the greatest help. That was a real turn in my Christian life and church life. In that year, 1934, Brother Nee entrusted more to me in the work. When he went away from Shanghai, he put his work upon my shoulders.

In October of 1934, he held a conference in Hangchow, a city beside the West Lake, and he spoke on God's overcomers. At the end of the conference, he got married, and he asked me to be his best man.

Brother Nee's Work from 1935-1939

In 1935 he had the burden to go to London to visit Brother T. Austin-Sparks. Before leaving for Europe, he first made arrangements in the summer to stay in my home in Chefoo. Eventually, he and Sister Nee stayed in my home. He had a conference there that brought in a deeper revival among us by speaking concerning Christ as the overcoming life. Then he canceled his scheduled trip to Europe. He returned to Shanghai to give a conference there. That was a great turn of the church life among us in 1935. Through the Lord's move at this time, the church life spread to other cities. In 1937 Brother Nee began to see that the co-workers needed to travel from one city to another to establish local churches. He then gave a series of messages firstly in January of 1937 in Shanghai to a small number of co-workers, among whom I was one. Then he repeated the same messages in October 1937 in Hankow. These were later put into the book entitled *The Normal Christian Church Life*. Then the war between China and Japan began, and he went out of the country to visit Europe in 1938 and 1939. He stayed in London about a year and a half, and he also visited the Scandinavian countries.

The Most Strategic Work of Brother Nee's Entire Life

In the summer of 1939, Brother Nee returned to China and had a conference on the Body of Christ. When he returned to Shanghai from England, he cabled me in northern China, asking me to come and attend his conference. I was traveling in north China with four young brothers to do the work of the Lord at that time, and we all went to Shanghai together. This conference was another great turning point in my life. Brother Nee stressed one thing again and again—the Body of Christ.

From that time in August 1939 through September 1942, Brother Nee had a conference in Shanghai nearly every month. Furthermore, Brother Nee would minister to the whole church in Shanghai every Wednesday night. He also spent several mornings each week with his trainees. For a period of time, I was there with him as a trainee. Not more than one hundred of us would meet with him in the mornings in Shanghai. During that time, he would ask us to give a testimony concerning how we had seen the Body. Hardly any had really seen the Body. After some gave a testimony, Brother Nee analyzed what they said, and pointed out all the major points to prove that they had not seen the Body. Someone may have said that they saw the Body, but their words exposed that they had never seen the Body. Those who were there were fully convinced that although they had the term *the Body*, they really had not seen it.

Brother Nee's fellowship on the Body during that time was the most strategic work of his entire life. From 1933 I was very close to Brother Nee. He put me in the position of bearing the ark with him, being "shoulder to shoulder" with him in the work. I knew what he was doing because I was always his helper. He and I often signed any announcements related to the work. I was observing him, and he was teaching me, fellowshipping with me, and letting me know all the things he was going to do. His most strategic work was during those years which he spent on the Body. Probably not since the time of the early apostles had there been messages given which were so solid, so profound, and so deep on the church as the Body. Many people may use the term *the Body*, and they may like to talk about Body ministry, but they really have not seen what the Body is.

In those years, Brother Nee also said that spiritual warfare is not an individual matter but a Body matter. In the Welsh revival of 1904 and 1905, the most useful one in the Lord's hand was Evan Roberts. In that revival he learned something concerning spiritual warfare, and he related his experiences to Jesse Penn-Lewis, and she put them into writing. Based on these experiences, she wrote a book entitled *War on the Saints*. Because she did not see that spiritual warfare is a Body matter, what she wrote in this book is not balanced. For this reason I would not advise anyone to read this book. Some who read this fellowship from Mrs. Penn-Lewis got into trouble with demons.

Most of these writings on spiritual warfare were translated by Brother Nee and put into his three-volume book *The Spiritual Man*. Later, he made clear publicly in the meetings that he regretted having included the chapter on spiritual warfare in this book, because that chapter was from the view of Evan Robert's individual experience. I told a publisher of this book that if he was going to print it, he should delete that chapter. That chapter was absolutely against Brother Nee's intention. From 1940 through 1942, he saw the Body and realized that spiritual warfare is not an individual matter but a Body matter. According to my own experience, before 1940 it was difficult to fight the spiritual warfare, but after we saw the Body, it was so easy to enter into this warfare.

The Rebellion against Brother Nee

Due to the exposure of the enemy's subtlety through Brother Nee's messages during those three years, the enemy caused a big turmoil in the church in Shanghai in 1942. Eventually, the church there was closed, and Brother Nee's ministry was stopped for six years. Some who did not know the real situation, said that Brother Nee was fully occupied with his pharmaceutical business during those six years, but this was absolutely not true. Strictly speaking, in those six years from June 1942 to 1948, he did not minister, not because he did not have the time but just because of the attack from the enemy. The enemy stirred up a rebellion against him. In 1945 he did speak in Chungking in western China. These messages are contained in the book entitled *The Orthodoxy of the Church*. These were the only messages he gave during those years.

The Recovery of Brother Nee's Ministry

The war ended in the Far East in August 1945. I was invited to go to Shanghai, and I stayed there from 1946 to the first part of 1949. In 1946 and 1947, I had much time with Brother Nee privately. I did my best to ask him to come back to his ministry to speak to us. I presented the need to him, but he told me that he could not and would not minister due to the rebellious spirit of some of the saints in Shanghai. The Lord eventually granted a big revival among us, and Brother Nee's ministry was recovered through that revival. Because his ministry was recovered, there was not only a revival but also a "big explosion" among us.

Six-month Training

During the time when his ministry was stopped, Brother Nee took the opportunity to buy many houses on a small mountain close to his hometown. Missionaries had built those houses for their summer retreat. During the war most of them left and were glad to sell those houses at a very cheap price. Brother Nee bought them with the intention of preparing for his coming training. Then the church in Shanghai was revived, and his ministry was recovered. In 1948 about eighty to one hundred saints went to this mountain to be with Brother Nee for a course of training which lasted about six months. Everybody was joyful in this training. They lived together day by day, praising, singing, praying, and coming to training meetings three times daily. Every day Brother Nee gave at least four or five messages, morning, afternoon, and evening. After that training, these eighty to one hundred saints came down from the mountain and were scattered throughout China. This caused a bigger explosion. In Tsingtao, the biggest city in my province, the church baptized seven hundred people in one day. That was in November 1948, one month after Brother Nee's six-month training course was finished.

Publishing Books before the Communist Takeover

Brother Nee intended to have a second training in 1949, in which I participated for a short time, but the Chinese Communists took over the country in that year, so we were scattered. As a rule, the Communists would give people two years of freedom after they took over a place, and they did the same thing with Brother Nee. He had two years of freedom in 1950 and 1951. In those two years, he did his best to publish as many books as possible because he anticipated that he would be arrested and put into prison. In 1952 he was arrested and put into prison for four years. In 1956 he was sentenced to fifteen years imprisonment, but from that day he remained in prison until he died in 1972. Thus, he was imprisoned for twenty years until his death. This fellowship gives us a brief sketch of Brother Nee's work.

In the next chapter we will fellowship concerning Brother Nee's sufferings. In all the years we were with him, we saw him pass through suffering after suffering. He was a man of suffering. He learned many strategic lessons from the Lord through his sufferings. We thank the Lord that through Brother Nee's sufferings, we received the help—the edification and the building up. He was a gift in life given by the Head to His Body.

CHAPTER SIX

THE HISTORY OF THE LOCAL CHURCHES

(4)

Scripture Reading: Rev. 2:2; 6:9b; 2:13-15, 20, 24; 3:2, 9, 15-18, 20; 17:4-6; 18:4

THE SPIRITUAL LESSONS LEARNED BY BROTHER NEE THROUGH HIS SUFFERINGS

In this chapter we want to begin seeing the spiritual lessons which Brother Nee learned through his sufferings. I was with Brother Nee for a long period of time. In my initial years in the work with him, especially in November and December of 1933 and January and February of 1934, he had many personal times with me to tell me many things concerning church history, his history, and the history of the Lord's work in China. His intention, of course, was to help me. He told me the lessons he learned through his sufferings. I could never forget the things he related to me because of the deep impression and great help which I received.

Learning to Live a Life of Faith through Poverty

The first thing Brother Nee suffered was poverty. He was enlightened to see that he had to serve the Lord by faith to fulfill the Lord's calling. He saw that he should not be hired by any mission, denomination, or person. He exercised a pure and single faith in God for his living (see *Watchman Nee's Testimony*, pp. 42-55). I followed Brother Nee in 1933 to take this way. Although this was very difficult, we learned the faithfulness of the Lord. The economic situation of China during that time was not good. In such a situation, we suffered poverty. Sometimes when Brother Nee was living in Shanghai in the early days of the church life, he had nothing to eat except a small amount of bread for the entire day. This happened a number of times, and I and other co-workers also suffered things like this. At times we did not know if we would eat our next meal. The Lord really did some miraculous things to take care of us.

In 1937 Brother Nee cabled us to come to him in Shanghai. I was assigned during that time to work in northern China, and Brother Nee had called a conference of all the co-workers in January to release the messages on the normal Christian church life. After we received his cable to come to that conference, we got on a train that took thirty-six hours to reach Shanghai. We traveled third class. The first-class compartment had places to sleep, but we did not have the money to pay for that. Brother Nee met us at the train station in Shanghai. After the conference of the co-workers in Shanghai, I was invited to minister in Hangchow. I was also invited to Nanking, the capital, and I traveled through many cities. I was away from home about two and a half months.

Because I left home in response to Brother Nee's urgent invitation, I did not have time or much money to arrange anything for my family. At that time we had four children. After I was gone about three or four weeks, my family ran out of food. My wife and some of the children knelt down and prayed for the next day's food. Not too long after they prayed, an old sister came to our house late in the night. This sister was well-off financially, but she did not love the Lord that much. She did not even attend the meetings regularly. She told my wife that while she was at home, there was something in her heart which caused her to have no rest. She felt that she had to come to my wife with an envelope. She gave the envelope to my wife and left. There was enough money in the envelope to meet the need of my family. This is an illustration of how the Lord took care of our need as we lived by faith in Him.

It was very hard to live by faith in God, without being hired by anyone, in the financial situation of China in those days. Brother Nee was the pioneer among us to take this way in all of China. The Lord Jesus really needed him and used him to cut and pave the way. Then we followed in his steps. Sometimes people would tell me, "You are just a follower of Watchman Nee." Although they said this to put me down, I felt wonderful and glorious.

Learning to Depend on the Lord and Live by the Resurrection Life through Ill Health

Brother Nee's sufferings also came from his ill health. He contracted tuberculosis in 1924, and by 1929 he was dying from this disease. Eventually, he received a word from Lord, he stood on that word, and he was healed. His testimony of this is in *Watchman Nee's Testimony*, pages 30-38. Later, he had stomach troubles, and then he had heart disease. He did not get married until 1934, and his ministry began about 1923. Eleven years of his ministry passed, and he did not have a wife to help him. He lived as a single man until 1934, so he really suffered.

He always told me beginning in 1934 that he could die at any time. Many times while he was speaking, he had to lean on the stand because he was in so much pain. He told us that many times, while he was speaking, he would break out in a cold sweat. Also, before he went to conference meetings, there were many times that he had to lay on the bed until the time came for him to speak. After he spoke, he immediately went back home to lie down. I believe that eventually in 1972 he died of his heart disease while he was in the communists' prison. We received definite information from a very close relative of his who was always taking care of him. He lived with heart disease for close to forty years. He was suffering all the time.

Through his poverty, he learned the lesson of faith. He knew how to be a "lily" (Matt. 6:28), living on this earth in total dependence upon God. He lived on this earth by faith in God, without trusting in any human help. Furthermore, because of his ill health, he had to learn to depend on the Lord. He learned to live by the resurrection life to meet his physical need. Many times he ministered, not by his physical strength or energy, but by the resurrection life. I saw this while he was speaking. Through all his sufferings, he learned some real lessons. I cannot estimate the tremendous help we received from these lessons. I personally received great help from his experiences.

The Spiritual Lessons Learned through Persecution from Christianity

In addition to his poverty and bad health, Brother Nee also suffered all kinds of persecution from Christianity. This is the third category of his sufferings. I would like to relate a little history so that we can see the background of Brother Nee's sufferings in this category. The Boxer Rebellion in China was in 1900. This was an attempt by some to drive foreigners out of China and to force Christians, both native and foreign, to renounce Christ. Afterward, there was a revolution in China, which succeeded in 1911. After 1911, there was no persecution of Christianity throughout all of China. Instead, many people began to have a positive attitude toward Christianity. As we have seen, Brother Nee was saved in 1920. That was during a time when Christianity had become prevailing. During that time the Lord was moving in the universities, and many young people were saved. Thus, there was not any persecution or opposition from the unbelievers. The persecution which Brother Nee suffered came almost entirely from Christianity.

Learning to Go outside the Camp to Bear the Lord's Reproach through Being Despised

First, many in Christianity despised him, even as a young man in his twenties. When Brother Nee was in his mid-twenties, he published the three volumes of *The Spiritual Man*. One top theologian commented that Brother Nee was merely a clever young man, who could pick up many things by reading English books and translating them into Chinese. Brother Nee was really despised. Being criticized is not as serious as being despised. Criticism "circumcises" us and "cuts us into pieces," but being despised is something more. Especially in those days, we were reminded of Hebrews 13:13: "Let us therefore go forth unto Him outside the camp, bearing His reproach." Together with Brother Nee, we were going to the Lord outside the camp to bear His reproach. We considered that reproach as the cross. The more we were despised, the happier we were because we were bearing the cross.

Learning to Deal with the Flesh through Being Criticized

Following being despised, Brother Nee was criticized by Christianity. He was criticized because he repudiated and renounced the entire unscriptural system of Christianity. In the twenty-four issues of his magazine *The Christian*, published in 1925 and 1926, Brother Nee "demolished" all of fallen Christianity. Some people today condemn me by saying that I am different from Watchman Nee. But what I have ministered cannot be compared in strength to what Brother Nee released to expose in detail the fallen situation of Christianity. Those in Christianity had to publish many things in criticism of him in order to defend themselves. I noticed that by being criticized, Brother Nee learned to deal with the flesh. He never reacted to criticism in a fleshly way. He learned the lesson of having his flesh dealt with.

Learning to Be Pure in Motive through Being Opposed

In addition to suffering criticism, Brother Nee was opposed by Christianity. One Christian publication in China opposed him in issue after issue. Following this opposition, they attacked Brother Nee. They did their best to put him down. By that time China was a constitutional country with the freedom of religion. Otherwise, even Brother Nee's life would have been in danger. The strongest attacks against him did not come from the native Christians but from the missionaries. The missionaries thought they had sacrificed their country, their homes, and so much for the Lord Jesus to go to a pagan country like China. They did this to help people be saved and to lay the foundation for and build up their mission churches. The Presbyterian missionaries built up the Presbyterian church, the Baptist missionaries built up the Baptist church, etc. They all built up their so-called churches.

Some of them would collect the people they had converted together, take a picture of them, and send that picture back to the mission board so that they could receive some money in return.

Then a young man named Watchman Nee rose up to expose the error of denominationalism. By ministering the truth of the Word, he demolished the divisive standing of the denominational churches built up by the missionaries. He declared that the denominational churches were wrong and that there should only be the church in a locality. Brother Nee said that he appreciated the missionaries bringing the Bible, the name of Christ, and the gospel to China, but he also said that they should not have come to build up their mission churches. He said that all the divisive names should be put aside, and that we should simply meet as the church, exalting only the name of Christ.

The circulation of his magazine, *The Christian*, went up to ten thousand subscriptions a month. Every month Brother Nee published ten thousand copies of this marvelous paper. This was why the missionaries attacked him so much. By being attacked, Brother Nee learned one lesson—to have his motive purified. He told me that when he was attacked by others, especially by the missionaries, he questioned himself. Since so many servants of the Lord attacked him, he considered that he might have been wrong. He appreciated that the missionaries had sacrificed so much to come to China to serve the Lord. By being attacked, he allowed himself to be checked by the Lord as to whether or not his motive was pure. He learned to deal with the Lord to be pure in motive.

One day he spoke to me concerning the purity of my motive. Whenever we were together, we never had loose talk or gossip. When he spoke to me concerning my motive, I believe he received the inspiration from the Lord to put me on the test. In the course of our fellowship, he suddenly asked me why I went to Hangchow. I was surprised and wondered why he asked me this since I had gone there a while before. I said, "I went there because I felt some of the brothers there needed my help. I went purposely to help them." He replied frankly to me, "You are just a politician." I told Brother Nee that I could not understand why he said this. I considered myself as a little servant who went there to serve the saints. How could he say that I was a politician? He replied, "Because you went to Hangchow with a purpose." I said, "My purpose was not bad. My purpose was to go there to help the saints." He said, "That is politics."

After Brother Nee said this, I wondered how I could serve the Lord again. Eventually, he helped me to understand that if one is going to a place, he should not have any purpose. Why do we go to a place? We go because the Lord leads us there. The Lord leads us to go, so we have to go. I may not be so clear what to do there, but the Lord knows. Thus, I am not going in a political way but in a pure way. Why am I going to a certain place? I am going because of the Lord's leading. What am I going to do there? I do not know, but He knows. This was a great lesson to me. I am still learning this lesson today. It is not easy to move in our service to the Lord without a purpose. Can we say that we move for the Lord without a purpose? According to Brother Nee, as long as you have a purpose, you are a politician. That was a hard lesson for me, but this helped me to always check my motive in my service. When we go somewhere it should be because of the Lord's initiation not ours. We should just follow the Lord's leading.

I received so much help from Brother Nee's fellowship with me that day. He paid a great price to learn such lessons, and he passed them on to us. When we were under his training, we did not learn mere doctrines. He told us all the time not to pick up mere doctrines but to learn some spiritual lessons. He helped us to realize that when we minister a teaching, that teaching must be full of reality according to our experiences.

Learning Not to Vindicate Ourselves through Evil Report from the Opposers and Persecutors

In addition to the attacks Brother Nee suffered, Christianity also spread rumors concerning him. Paul called these rumors an "evil report" in 2 Corinthians 6:8. The opposers did their best to defame Brother Nee. I would like to relate an illustration of the many false rumors concerning him. One day Miss Barber's co-worker, Miss Gross, came to visit Brother Nee. By that time, Miss Barber had gone to the Lord, but Miss Gross still lived in Shanghai. She heard some rumors about Brother Nee, and she came to see him. Brother Nee was single at that time, and Miss Gross, along with Miss Barber, had helped him spiritually. Miss Gross had the position to rebuke him. She spoke to him in a rebuking tone and said, "I heard that you have a woman living with you." Brother Nee answered, "Yes." Then Miss Gross said unhappily, "How could you do such a thing?" She was very disappointed and left after a short time. As Brother Nee related this story to me, he said, "Witness, do you know who was staying with me? That woman was my mother. Because I was so sick, my mother came from a distance to take care of me. Then the rumor went out that I had a woman living with me. Yes, I did have a woman living with me." Being bothered, I asked Brother Nee why he did not tell Miss Gross that his mother was staying with him. He said, "She didn't ask me who the woman was." Then he said, "Witness, we have to learn never to say anything to vindicate ourselves. We should just tell people the truth." When Miss Gross confronted him by asking if a woman was living with him, all Brother Nee said was "yes." He was learning the lesson not to vindicate himself, so he had to suffer the rebuking from Miss Gross. He said, "If she would have asked me who was living with me, I would have told her. But she did not ask, so I did not need to tell her. If I had told her, I would have been vindicating myself."

This shows us how Brother Nee, through his sufferings, was a man who was always learning spiritual lessons from the Lord. I believe that in this century he became the most useful vessel in the Lord's eyes. We have seen that in 1942 the enemy stirred up a big rebellion against him. Nearly all the co-workers and leading ones were against Brother Nee. There was a saying then that only "two and a half" persons among the co-workers and leading ones were not opposing him—one sister and "one and a half" brothers. I was the one brother of this "one and a half." I told people that I did not care how much they told me Brother Nee was wrong. I could never forget the lessons I learned from him. I was with him day by day for a long period of time. I could never deny the solid things he learned and passed on to me. I did not care what others said about him. Some in Christianity said to me, "You are just following a man—Watchman Nee." I said that it was a glory to me that I could have such a man from the Lord to follow.

The Lord's Vindication

Although there was so much opposition to Brother Nee within Christianity, there was also some vindication from the Lord. In 1938 and 1939 he was in England, and he was invited to the Keswick convention, a gathering of Christians who were very much for the inner life. The chairman of the convention had heard something concerning Watchman Nee, so he asked Brother Nee to come up to the platform to give a prayer. In those days to be asked to be a speaker or to give a prayer at the Keswick convention was a great thing. Brother Nee was hesitant about giving such a public prayer, but Brother T. Austin-Sparks, who had brought him to the convention, encouraged him to do it. Thus, Brother Nee went to the platform and prayed. His prayer taught the entire congregation. After his prayer, there was a message. After the message, however, no one talked about the message but about Watchman Nee's prayer.

At that time Brother Nee was also able to have some real fellowship with the chairman of the convention, who was also the chairman of the best mission that went to China, the China Inland Mission. In their fellowship, this brother entirely agreed with Brother Nee. He told Brother Nee that what the Lord had commissioned him to do in China was according to Hudson Taylor's burden. He was sorry that their missionaries had wrongly opposed Brother Nee. This brother later went to China purposely. He called all of the China Inland Mission missionaries together to Shanghai and told them openly that they were wrong to oppose the ministry of Watchman Nee. He told them that what Brother Nee was doing was exactly what they should do. He also shared that because they had failed the Lord, the Lord raised up Brother

Nee to replace them. He advised them and begged them not to oppose or attack Brother Nee anymore. Regretfully, after he left, the missionaries attacked Brother Nee even more.

From 1927 when Brother Nee established the church in Shanghai until the day he died, he was only invited to speak to a denomination once. This was in 1932 in my hometown. He went there, and he stayed in my home. That was the first time we met. In one sense, he was very unpopular. In another sense, he was popular in being attacked by Christianity.

THE FOCUS OF BROTHER NEE'S MINISTRY— CHRIST AS LIFE FOR THE CHURCH

Today some publish Brother Nee's books on the spiritual side of Christ being life to us, but they will not publish his material on the practical side concerning the church. Because the books concerning Christ as life have helped thousands, Brother Nee has a popular name today. But this was absolutely against his intention. He never would agree with this. For this reason we have done our best to publish Brother Nee's fellowship concerning the church.

Some even spread a rumor that after World War II, Watchman Nee changed his concept concerning the church and the denominations, but the book entitled *Further Talks on the Church Life* disproves this. The messages in this book were all given by Brother Nee after the war. The earliest one was in 1948, and the last one was in 1951. These messages prove that Brother Nee never changed his concept. After the war, I was working closely with him for at least two and a half years, and he told me what was on his heart. He said that we are not here just for Christ but for Christ and His Body, the church. He said that our vision is not just Christ as life but Christ as life for the church. He always ministered on Christ and the church. Many times in 1947 and 1948, he opened up his heart to me personally or to me and Sister Peace Wang, an elderly co-worker.

Some have also made the accusation that Witness Lee is different from Watchman Nee. One author accused me of going beyond Brother Nee by allegorizing the Bible. He accused me of going too far by saying in the book *The Glorious*

Church that Eve is a type of the church. The author of this accusation, however, did not realize that *The Glorious Church* was written by Brother Nee. In his intention to show people that I was different from Brother Nee, in the Lord's sovereignty, he made me the same as Brother Nee. Brother Nee's ministry was always focused on Christ as life for the building up of the organic Body of Christ, and we have always continued in this focus.

CHAPTER SEVEN

THE HISTORY OF THE LOCAL CHURCHES

(5)

Scripture Reading: John 7:39a; 14:6-11, 16-21, 23, 26; 16:7, 13-15; 17:21, 23; 20:22; 1 John 3:24b; 4:13

In the previous chapter, we saw the lessons which Brother Nee learned through his sufferings. We have covered his suffering from poverty, from ill health, and from Christianity. His suffering from Christianity includes five items: being despised, being criticized, being opposed, being attacked, and being spoken of evilly through rumors. The most subtle and damaging item is rumors. Satan is a liar and the father of all the liars (John 8:44). A rumor is a lie. Brother Nee had to endure many rumors about him throughout his ministry. Such suffering came to him from those in Christianity.

In May of 1934, he and I were traveling together to a suburban city outside of Shanghai named Kiangwang. While he was driving, he turned to me and said, "Brother, now we have to turn to the Gentiles." He was quoting Paul's word in Acts 13:46 after being rejected by the Jews. Paul and Barnabas preached the gospel to the Jews, but the Jews rejected them and persecuted them. Since the Jews rejected Paul's ministry, he said, "Behold, we turn to the Gentiles." By 1934 when Brother Nee said this to me, his ministry had been fully rejected by Christianity. He presented his ministry to Christianity, but in return he received despising, criticizing, opposing, attacking, and rumors. Then he told me that we had to turn to the Gentiles. From that time we started to pay more attention to bringing unbelieving sinners into the church. In this chapter we want to go on to see another category of Brother Nee's sufferings.

BROTHER NEE'S SUFFERINGS
FROM WITHIN THE CHURCH

Being Unjustly Excommunicated

Brother Nee's sufferings from certain ones among us were more serious than those from Christianity. As we have pointed out, the church life began in Brother Nee's hometown in 1922. In 1924 he was excommunicated by six brothers. This was carried out not just by an announcement in the meeting but by something in writing, and it happened while he was away. He related the whole story of his being excommunicated to me in detail.

He was working in the city of Hangchow, which is very close to Shanghai, when he received a letter telling him that he was excommunicated. Brother Nee told me that when he was about to react to this, the Lord checked with him, "Are you going to be in My hand, or are you going to be in your own hand?" Thus, Brother Nee had no choice in this matter. After his preaching work was finished, he returned to his hometown. Most of the brothers and sisters there were students saved through him, and they were furious about what had happened. They absolutely did not agree with what was done to Brother Nee. They went to the pier to wait for the arrival of his boat. When he arrived, they told him that he should not stand for this excommunication and that he had to do something. He was seasick from his journey, so he told them to come to his home that night to have fellowship about this matter.

That night his home was crowded with people. But before they came, he had received a word from the Lord telling him not to vindicate himself and to leave the city the next day. He told the young people gathered at his house, "I cannot do anything because the Lord will not allow me to do it. The only thing I can do is to get packed and leave the city tomorrow." They were so disappointed, and many of them wept when Brother Nee said this. He left Foochow in 1924 and went to Pagoda. Brother Nee wrote a marvelous and inspiring hymn during that time. This long hymn, which has not yet been translated into English, speaks of a man learning how to bear the cross without vindicating himself, learning how to suffer without saying anything. This is a long hymn which relates his feeling and sensation during that time.

Later he received the burden to put out the monthly magazine called *The Christian*. The issues of this publication covered the truths revealed in Revelation 1—3 and Genesis 1. Brother Nee wrote these under severe suffering in 1925 and 1926. At the end of this period of time, he had the burden to go to Shanghai and Nanking to start a new work there. The church in Shanghai was established at the end of 1926 and the beginning of 1927.

We need to see a principle from looking at Brother Nee's life. This principle is that the church is produced by the life of Christ through sufferings. The birth of the church is like the travail of a mother who is delivering a child. We should not think that we can go to a place to establish a church in an easy way. The church is produced by the life of Christ through someone's sufferings.

Suffering from Dissenting Ones

From the beginning of the church life in mainland China, there was a sister who was dissenting toward Brother Nee. She was about twenty-five or twenty-six when Brother Nee was twenty years old. She was a gifted sister who eventually became a traveling preacher and was considered very highly by Christianity. Following the six brothers who excommunicated Brother Nee, she was the major one who was always dissenting toward him. In January of 1934, while we were in the third Victory Conference in Shanghai, she was in the meetings in a dissenting way. While Brother Nee was speaking, she was shaking her head in disagreement. She was older than him and received respect from many directions, yet she was dissenting toward him. I saw many dissenting ones throughout the years. This sister was one of the strongest of these dissenting ones. She was in the church life in the beginning in China, but eventually she left. Such dissenting ones were a real suffering to Brother Nee.

Suffering from Others'
Immaturity and Incompetence

Brother Nee also suffered because of the immaturity and incompetence of those around him. He was bearing the responsibility with the brothers, but there was no comparison between him and all the other brothers. He was very mature and competent, but the others were immature and incompetent. In the early days of the Lord's recovery in mainland China, Brother Watchman Nee was a unique, extraordinary person. Spiritually, he was far beyond the other brothers. He saw many things which the brothers did not see. Most of us do not realize much concerning this kind of suffering. Suppose that a brother who is thirty-four years old had to serve and bear responsibility with a brother who is only fifteen years old. This illustration may give us some idea of Brother Nee's suffering in this regard.

Because of the immaturity of the brothers, Brother Nee also had to endure their stubbornness. The practice of the church life in China began in 1922, and I came into the work in a practical way in 1933. Before I entered into the work with Brother Nee, I went to visit him in Shanghai for four months. At the end of that four-month period, Brother Nee said to me, "Witness, we brothers feel that you should move your family here and stay with us so that we can work together. Please open to the Lord concerning this matter." I went to the Lord, and I became clear that I had to move to Shanghai.

When I entered into the work with Brother Nee, he put me into a position of bearing the responsibility with him. At first I wondered why he did this since I could be considered as a "new hand" in the work. A few of the others had been in Shanghai with Brother Nee for six or seven years. I was a new person in the work, but I was immediately brought into such a heavy responsibility with Brother Nee. Then I found out that all the other brothers were busy taking care of their jobs and businesses. Only one brother there was a co-worker. Whereas I was two years younger than Brother Nee, this brother was about seven years older than him.

Before this brother came into the Lord's work, he had been a postmaster.

I would like to relate something that happened with this brother to show you how Brother Nee suffered. One day a learned man was saved among us, and he desired to be baptized before he left China for the United States. Brother Nee was so clear about this newly saved one, and he agreed that this man should be baptized before he left China. However, the brother who had been a postmaster did not agree with Brother Nee. Brother Nee asked this co-worker what he was concerned about. He said that he was concerned that this new one might not be saved. Then Brother Nee said that if something was mistaken, he would be willing to bear all the responsibility before the Lord. The co-worker still would not agree to this new one being baptized. Brother Nee had shared previously in some messages that in the church life we always need the fellowship and that we should not do things individualistically. Because Brother Nee insisted on doing everything in fellowship, he would not baptize this new one without the co-worker's agreement. Thus, the new one left China without being baptized. This is just one of the cases of Brother Nee's suffering because of the immaturity of those with him.

I would like to relate another case of his suffering in this matter. I have shared that Brother Nee picked up many positive things from the different practices in Christianity. At the beginning of the church life, he picked up the way to have our meetings mostly from the practice of the Brethren. This is why some people called us the Chinese version of the Brethren movement. At the beginning, we practiced our meetings more than seventy percent according to the Brethren way. In the meetings of the Brethren, the sisters were not allowed to utter anything. They were allowed to sing, but they were not allowed to speak or even to pray.

By 1933 when I came into the work, Brother Nee realized that not having the sisters pray in the meetings was a big loss to the church. He became clear that it is absolutely right for the sisters to pray in the meetings (see 1 Cor. 11:5 and note 2 of 1 Cor. 14:34—Recovery Version). The leading sisters agreed with Brother Nee, but most of the so-called leading ones believed that the sisters should not utter anything. Brother Nee fellowshipped with them that we should release the sisters in the meetings to pray, but nearly all the brothers said "no." When Brother Nee proposed this, I said "amen," but I was considered by the others as a newcomer who did not know much. This is another example of Brother Nee's sufferings.

The beginning of the practice of the church life in China was difficult. Brother Nee was the "first traveler" who paid the price to cut the way for the church life. Now that the cutting has been accomplished, it is easy for us to travel on the "road" of the church life. Brother Nee was the "road cutter." He placed me so close to him in the work because he was lonely. By the Lord's mercy, my spirit was strong to say "amen" to Brother Nee. That became a joy to him in the midst of his suffering. I hope that we would learn the spiritual lessons through this fellowship.

Suffering from Others' Ambition for Position

Brother Nee also suffered from those who were ambitious for position. Because his health was not good, he often was not able to attend the meetings. He worked on his publications and took care of the conferences, but mostly he could not take care of the meetings of the church on a regular basis. He turned over the responsibility of all the meetings to me. When I was new in the work, there was a brother among us who was very active and aggressive, expressing that he loved the Lord so much. I appreciated that brother, and I asked him to give a message in one of the Lord's Day afternoon meetings. At that time we had three meetings on the Lord's Day—in the morning, afternoon, and evening. Brother Nee found out about this and told me that I should not have asked that brother to give a message. I was wondering what was wrong. Brother Nee did not tell me at that time.

Eventually, I came to know the situation with that brother. He was the third one to come into the church life in Shanghai. The second one was Dr. Yu, the eye specialist, and the first one was the brother who had been a postmaster. These three brothers all came out of the China Inland Mission in Shanghai. That was a strong reason why the Shanghai missionaries went against Brother Nee. These three were the top ones who were gained by that mission.

From 1927 when this particular brother came into the church, he was always ambitious to be one of the elders, but he truly was not qualified. He was not that kind of person, so Brother Nee would not agree with his being a leading one. Eventually, in 1948 after he had been in the church life for twenty-one years, he left the church and caused a division. He started a meeting in his home and hired a traveling preacher, similar to what Micah did in Judges 17 in hiring someone to be his priest.

I saw a number of brothers who passed through the church life, expecting to receive some position. Brother Nee always told people that the church is not an organization with position but an organism with living members. Anything that is positioned on a person's physical body, such as false teeth, is an inorganic item which is foreign to the body. Nearly all the famous preachers among the Chinese who were around my age passed through the Lord's recovery in China. They came and met with us for a while, expecting to receive some position in the work. Eventually, they found out that there was no position for them, so they left and became opposers. Brother Nee told us publicly that whoever desires a position in the church life will never get that position.

There was another brother among us who pretended to be the most spiritual person to fulfill his ambition. At the beginning, nearly the whole church in Shanghai was fooled by this young brother, but gradually the "fox tails" came out, one by one. All the responsible brothers believed that he was very spiritual, and some of them even felt shameful that they were not as spiritual as he was. Eventually, however, this young man was exposed. The leading ones and the co-workers came to know that he was false, and they all agreed to deal with him. He was ambitious, pretending to be something that he was not. The church called an urgent meeting, and the whole congregation came together. In this meeting one of the co-workers announced something concerning this brother's falsehood, and many others also stood up to condemn him. He was condemned by the entire congregation. Then he left and became another cause of division. After he left, he was hired to be a teacher by the top women's seminary in China.

Whenever trouble came among us, the "arrows" always went to Brother Nee. He was the target. At that time none of the arrows came to me because I was not qualified to be the target. I was under the protection of a big "umbrella," and that umbrella was Brother Nee. Sometimes when people attacked him, they would highly appraise me. Within myself I realized their subtlety. I realized that if Brother Nee were gone, their arrows would be shot at me.

I want to say something for the sake of the young brothers. The ambition of the brothers is a problem in the church. It is a shame to say this, but it is a fact. This ambition caused Brother Nee much suffering. Brother Nee told us that no one ever gave him a position and that he had no position to give others. Eventually, those who were ambitious for position left. Some of the divisions were caused by this kind of ambition. The ambitious ones would never admit that they were ambitious. When they caused a division, they did it with a certain excuse. They put on a "cloak" of a certain doctrine. They would say that the church was wrong in this certain doctrine, and because they were clear about this they had to leave. This was altogether a pretense, an excuse, and a cloak for their ambition.

Suffering Rebellion from Those among Us

Brother Nee also suffered attacks from rebellious ones who were among us. When I was younger, I read the stories about the children of Israel rebelling against Moses. When I came into the church life, I saw such rebellion. Brother Nee suffered not only the attacks from the outsiders but also the attacks and rebellion from those inside the church life.

I would like to present an example of such attacks suffered by Brother Nee. There was a co-worker among us who fell into immorality. The local leading ones could not handle the situation, so they referred the case to Brother Nee. Brother

Nee was forced to deal with this situation, and this brother had to be removed from the fellowship of the church. Later this brother, who had been a co-worker, started to attack Brother Nee. Eventually, he went to Hong Kong to set up another meeting, which was another division. That meeting was set up close to Brother K. H. Weigh's home, but it did not last too long because this rebellious brother eventually died of cancer.

Before he died, he attacked Brother Nee. This was during the Second World War when Shanghai was taken over by the Japanese army. The Japanese army was afraid of the Communists. When they found out that someone was a Communist, they killed him. At that time the Japanese military police were careful to examine all the mail. When this rebellious brother was in Hong Kong, he sent Brother Nee materials concerning communism so that the Japanese military would think Brother Nee was a communist and arrest him. Brother Nee, however, was under the protection of the Lord, and this mail that was sent to him several times was never discovered.

Suffering Defamation
and Evil Report from Opposers

Brother Nee suffered such attacks from rebellious ones many times. In 1950 Brother Nee came out of China to Hong Kong for the last time. In Hong Kong we were holding meetings every evening. One night when Brother Nee and I walked out of the meeting hall, there were some people standing at the entrance distributing some booklets against him. Some of these booklets were passed to him. He smiled a little bit and did not take them. They were filled with false rumors and other defamatory things that were absolutely against him. This is another illustration of the attacks he suffered.

The Suffering Related to His Marriage

I would like to relate one more complicated case which caused Brother Nee to suffer greatly. This case was related to his marriage. By 1934 at the age of thirty-two, Brother

Nee was still not married. The circumstances surrounding his marriage became a difficult situation for him. He was married to Sister Charity Chang, Brother Samuel Chang's sister, on October 19, 1934, the day after a ten-day conference.

A short while after Brother Nee's wedding, there was a big turmoil. This turmoil came from two directions. The first direction was from Brother Chang's aunt. Brother Chang and his sisters lost their parents when they were young, and they were under the care of their aunt. His aunt did not agree with her niece marrying such a "poor preacher." At that time in China, a preacher was looked upon as a poor beggar, especially by those of the higher class. Although the aunt would not agree with the marriage, her niece, Charity, was very much for Brother Nee, so they were married. After their marriage, the aunt continued to oppose. Some of those in Christianity found out about this and joined with her. This was the second direction of the turmoil.

One day Brother Nee came to me and told me that according to his knowledge there had never been such a problem with someone's wedding. Their names were even in the biggest newspaper in Shanghai. After he had this time with me, I could not find him for a few days. Eventually, I found out that he went far away from Shanghai to another province.

Having His Ministry Stopped for Six Years because of Rebellion among the Saints

Now I would like to share about the biggest "storm" in the churches in China. In order to understand why this storm occurred, we need to know the background of the situation in China at that time. In the early days of the Lord's recovery in China, the financial situation among the Chinese was not good. Still, a number of saints were raised up to serve the Lord by faith.

I would like to share a personal testimony as an example of the way we lived. In 1936 I was sent by the work to northern China to work in Tientsin, close to Peking, the capital. In those days the work would send people without supplying them with anything for their need. If there was the feeling for someone to go somewhere, they went by faith, without help from the work for their material supply. That was our practice in the early days.

When I was in Tientsin, I realized that I needed a bicycle to help me travel in such a large city. I had a little over forty dollars, just enough money to bring my wife and three children from my hometown to join me. I went to the Lord to ask Him how He felt about my purchasing a bicycle. I was so clear within that the Lord wanted me to have one although I did not have any money to buy it. The Lord gave me the assurance within that He would meet this need. This took place on Saturday.

On the Lord's Day after the Lord's table, I received a designated gift of two dollars that had been placed in the offering box. The next day an older brother came to see me. Before he left he put an envelope on my table, saying, "Brother Lee, this is for you." Then he left. There was ten dollars in that envelope. Later some registered mail came to me with a twenty-dollar money order from a city far away.

I asked a young brother, who had lost his job and was staying with me, if he would go with me to the post office to get this money order cashed. He agreed. On our way to the post office, I saw a bicycle store. I went in this store and saw a bicycle for sale that seemed very appropriate. The owner said that it would cost me a total of thirty-two dollars. I agreed to buy it, and he promised to deliver the bicycle to me in the evening. After getting the money order cashed at the post office, we returned home.

In the evening, the store delivered the bicycle. I went to my room to kneel down, pray, and thank the Lord. While I was thanking the Lord, He impressed me within to count how much money I had received since the Lord's Day evening. Two dollars from the offering box, ten dollars from a brother, and a money order for twenty dollars totaled exactly thirty-two dollars! When I realized what the Lord had done, I thanked Him with tears for His faithfulness. This was the way we co-workers lived by faith in the early days of the Lord's recovery in China.

Many were raised up to serve the Lord full-time, but the financial situation was not that good. As a result, the co-workers had to pass through many trials of poverty, and many became sick. In one meeting Brother Nee told us that about one-third of our co-workers had died of tuberculosis. I pointed out in a previous chapter that Brother Nee used one-third of his income to support others for the Lord's work, but the need among us was great. Brother Nee's second brother was an expert in pharmaceutical chemistry, and he began to produce some medicine in China. He did not know how to manage, so he asked Brother Nee to do it. Brother Nee took that as an opportunity to do some business in order to supply the Lord's work.

He was in this business a little over two years, from 1940 to 1942. Then there was a misunderstanding among the brothers. I would say that this mostly came from ambition. Some of the brothers who were working in the pharmaceutical factory were ambitious for higher position. The misunderstanding became bigger and bigger and developed to such an extent that the entire church in Shanghai became rebellious toward Brother Nee with a few exceptions.

At the same time, the Japanese military police were there trying to arrest Brother Nee. This situation forced the church in Shanghai to "close its doors." The Japanese military police attempted to force the church in Shanghai to join the false Christianity association under the Japanese military police. The church could not do this. Also, within the church there was a big turmoil against Brother Nee. Thus, the church had no way to go on.

Brother Nee was wise to flee and escape from Shanghai. Otherwise, he would have been arrested by the Japanese military police. He went to the interior of China and carried on his pharmaceutical factory in Chungking, the capital of China during the war. Brother Samuel Chang was a great help to Brother Nee in that pharmaceutical factory. Due to the great turmoil in the church in Shanghai, Brother Nee had no other choice but to stop his ministry. His ministry was stopped for six years. There was a rumor that he was too occupied with his pharmaceutical business and did not have the time to minister. This was false. He did not minister because of the rebellion. This was the last and greatest suffering which Brother Nee had to endure before his imprisonment.

In 1948 a big revival was brought in among us, and Brother Nee returned to his ministry. Through that revival nearly all the rebellious ones repented to him. Though many had become rebellious toward Brother Nee, they were not against the church. It was a real testimony that almost everyone stayed with the church and did not go back to the denominations. During the time of the rebellion, some went to Brother Nee and encouraged him to set up another meeting. He said that this should not be done. He told these saints that regardless of whether the church was against him or for him, it was still the church, and they had to continue in the church.

When Brother Nee returned to his ministry, there was a bigger revival. The church then decided to buy a big piece of land for a meeting hall that could seat three thousand inside and two thousand outside. The price of the land was about one hundred thousand dollars, and the price to build the meeting hall was about the same. I was bearing the responsibility in these financial matters. One day Brother Nee's wife told me that he wanted me to go to his home that night. When I went to his home, he handed over to me thirty-seven gold bars at ten ounces each. This was three hundred seventy ounces of gold at fifty dollars an ounce at that time. He said, "Take this and use it for the payment of the land." He told me he got it from the pharmaceutical business.

After the revival brought in through the return of Brother Nee to his ministry, he began to have a training. Later the Communists took over his training center. He was arrested in 1952 and was imprisoned until his death twenty years later.

According to my view and knowledge of Brother Nee, he did not have much peace in his life. He suffered his entire life. He was really a suffering person. In all his sufferings, he learned to deal with his natural life and self. The last lesson he learned through being put aside from the ministry for six years was the breaking of the outer man and the release of the spirit. He learned this one lesson in those six years. During this time he would not minister because so many were rebellious toward him, but some of us had many times of fellowship with him. He always talked to us about the breaking of our outer man and the release of our spirit. Those six years of suffering helped him to learn the lesson of having the natural man broken. When the natural man is broken, the release of the spirit is possible.

He did not merely pass on teaching and doctrines to people. All of his teaching had the backing of real experience learned through sufferings. He was not just a Bible student, who learned doctrines and passed them on to others. Whatever he ministered, he himself experienced. He learned so much through all his sufferings. Praise the Lord! Today we are the ones who inherit all the lessons. The sufferings I saw with Brother Nee and the lessons he learned through them helped my life very much. I can never forget what I saw in him. All the impressions I received of him became the greatest help to my Christian life. This is also a great help to the churches. Today we have such a heritage, which was built up by one who paid such a great price. The price was the sufferings. Brother Nee was a man of suffering. He did not have any children, and his wife went to the Lord about seven or eight months before he died in prison. There was no need for him to write a will because he had nothing left when he went to the Lord. However, he left much with us. Today we have the churches and such a rich heritage.

Chapter Eight

THE HISTORY OF THE LOCAL CHURCHES

(6)

Scripture Reading: 2 Cor. 4:1, 5; 3:5-6, 8; Phil. 1:20-21a; Col. 1:25-28; Eph. 3:8-11; 5:32

In the previous two chapters, we saw the sufferings of Brother Nee and the spiritual lessons he learned through them. The Gospels show us that the Lord Jesus also suffered persecution from the religious Jews. They despised Him, criticized Him, opposed Him, and attacked Him. They also spread evil and false rumors concerning Him. The book of Acts and the Epistles show that the Judaizers persecuted the apostles in the same way. Today the religious people also persecute the real followers of the Lord in His recovery. They despise, criticize, oppose, attack, and spread false rumors about those who follow the Lord in His recovery.

Besides enduring such attacks from Christianity, we have seen that Brother Nee also suffered from certain ones among us. He was unjustly excommunicated, and he suffered from dissenting ones. The dissenting ones may say something good about the leading ones or the church, but what they say positively is always followed by the word *but*. They may say, "Brother John is such a good brother who ministers life to people, but...." What comes after the word *but* is always negative.

Brother Nee also suffered from others' immaturity and incompetence. The immature ones do not like to labor; they like to talk. In an office, some people do not work properly, but they talk a lot. In the church life, those who are laborers do not talk much. The ones who talk much do not labor much. The apostle Paul calls such people "busybodies" (2 Thes. 3:11; 1 Tim. 5:13). There is a difference between talkers and workers. In the beginning of the church life, I was somewhat deceived by the talkers. I thought they loved the Lord so much because they expressed so much concern for the Lord's work. Eventually, I found out that these talkers were not genuine. The immature and incompetent ones are very talkative, and Brother Nee suffered from such ones.

He also suffered from the brothers' stubbornness, their unwillingness to say "amen" to his leading from the Lord. We have to learn, on the one hand, to suffer others' stubbornness, but on the other hand, to drop our stubbornness. We should always learn to go along with the brothers. We should not trust in ourselves so much. Instead, we must learn to trust in our brothers and sisters. We have also seen that Brother Nee suffered from others' ambition for position and from rebellion among the saints.

BROTHER NEE'S MINISTRY

The Ministry Produced by Revelation and Suffering

Now that we have seen something concerning the revelations Brother Nee received from the Lord and his sufferings, we want to see something concerning his ministry. Following the sufferings is the ministry. The ministry comes out of revelation plus suffering. Without revelation, a person cannot have any ministry because he has nothing with which to minister. But if a person has revelation without suffering, he still does not have a ministry. He may have a gift to teach, but there is a great difference between a gift and a ministry. The ministry is something higher, deeper, and more valuable. A gift in itself may be superficial, low, and cheap.

If we have the revelation, God will put us into the furnace, the oven, so that we can pass through the sufferings. Through the sufferings, we learn the real lessons in life. Then we will have the ministry. We all have to be deeply impressed with these two things—revelation and suffering. The ministry comes out of revelation and suffering.

The book of Acts and the Epistles of Paul show us his sufferings (Col. 1:24). We know by Paul's writings that before he passed through the sufferings, he received revelations

(2 Cor. 12:1, 7). He firstly received the revelations, but this does not mean that after receiving them he immediately went out to eloquently pass on his knowledge to people. If he had done this, it would not have been the ministry. What he shared would have been merely a teaching or an exercise of his gift, but not the ministry. We know, however, that the apostle Paul was not like this. After he received the revelations of the Lord, the Lord put him into the oven, into the fire, to be burned, to suffer. In his writings we see the sequence of the revelations first and then the sufferings. Then the ministry came out of these two things.

The revelation has to be burned into us. We may use the illustration of making a certain kind of porcelain vase. An artist may paint a picture on the vase, but the vase then needs to be burned. Then the picture is burned into the vase. After the picture has been burned into the vase, it can never be erased because it is one with the vase. Our receiving the revelation may be compared to the vase receiving the picture. But after this the revelation needs to be burned into us in order to make the revelation one with us. To receive revelation is one thing; to be burned with the revelation is another thing.

The revelation is burned into us by suffering. No real minister of God can avoid suffering. This is impossible. We all need it. How much life and how much reality of the riches of Christ we can minister depends upon two elements—how much revelation we have received plus how much we have suffered for what has been revealed to us. Suffering has to be added to revelation. Then we have a ministry.

In all the Epistles, we can see three things—the revelation, the suffering, and the ministry. Then there is the work. The work comes not out of the teaching or the gift, but out of the ministry. Paul said that he had received this ministry (2 Cor. 4:1) and that he was made a minister of the new covenant (2 Cor. 3:6). Today the word *minister* has been spoiled because of being misused in Christianity. We have to realize what a minister is. A minister is one who has a real ministry which was created with two things—revelation plus suffering.

The Difference between the Gifts and the Ministry

We may ask what the difference is between the gifts and the ministry. The book of Numbers records how Balaam's donkey spoke a human language (22:28). Was that a ministry? That was not a ministry but a gift. This difference may also be illustrated by a Chinese person who speaks both Chinese and English. Because the Chinese language has been wrought into him, he speaks in Chinese spontaneously without effort. Because Chinese has been constituted into him, his speaking in Chinese is a "ministry." Because English has not been wrought into him, his speaking in English is a "gift."

What is a ministry? A ministry is the expression of what you are. To minister is to express what you are. To exercise a gift, though, may be a performance. When a man walks, moves, acts, and speaks, he expresses what he is. His expression of what he is, is his "ministry." A monkey can sometimes be trained to act like a man, but that is just a performance. That is a "gift." In today's Christianity there are many performances.

If the apostle Paul were to stay with us for a month, we would see that he himself is what he ministers. Paul was really what he ministered because what he had seen was wrought into his being. Eventually, he ministered what he was. The person was the message. In today's Christianity, a person may be merely eloquent and learned. His speaking may even be with a certain kind of religious tone. That is a performance. It is not the real thing. Paul, however, was different.

I came to know some famous Christian workers who talked much about the lessons of the cross. When I was with them, though, I did not see these lessons. My experience with Brother Nee was different. I was with him for over eighteen years. Sometimes he spoke about the cross, but I saw the cross in him. The sufferings that came to him from many directions were the working of the cross. The cross had been worked into Brother Nee. What he ministered was not merely a teaching by a gift. What he had was a ministry, and that ministry was what he was.

We should not appreciate the gifts so much. It was

miraculous for Balaam's donkey to speak a human language, but we should not be overly excited about something like that. Instead, we have to gain the proper ministry. Then we will minister what we are to people. Our eloquence and our gift mean very little. It is easy for the devil to take advantage of our eloquence and gift to cheat us. We should not trust or appreciate our eloquence, our gift, or our talent. We may admire a certain person because he is so talented, but to be talented alone is terrible. In order to build up the church, we do not need mere gifts and teachings. We need the ministry. We need brothers and sisters who have been burned with some things revealed by God. Then they will have the ministry.

When a person has a ministry, he may not need to speak very much. His very presence ministers life to people. His presence in a meeting means much. If he is there, the meeting will be rich. If he is absent, the meeting will have a lack. Even his silent presence in the meetings makes a difference because he is a person who has a real ministry. He does not have mere teachings, knowledge, or gifts, but something of God in eternity has been wrought into his being. The presence of such a person makes a difference.

When the saints bring their troubles and problems into the presence of such a person, sometimes there is no need for him to say a word and the problems will be solved. I saw this in the past. When the saints bring their problems into such a person's presence, they receive the light. This person's presence becomes the light because light has been wrought into his being. When others are in his presence, they are under the enlightening. They see light in his light. Today in the church we need the ministry. Brother Nee always belittled and even condemned the gifts. He always stressed the ministry again and again.

First and Second Corinthians show the distinction between the gifts and the ministry. The first Epistle deals negatively with the gifts; the second speaks positively about the ministry. The church needs the ministry much more than the gifts. In the first Epistle to the Corinthians, Paul depreciated the gifts. In the second Epistle, the ministry is emphasized again and again. We have received this ministry, and this ministry is the ministry of the Spirit and of life (2 Cor. 3:6, 8). What is needed in the churches today is the ministry, not the gifts. After receiving the revelation, Brother Nee passed through many sufferings. Then the ministry came out of him. He had the ministry.

The Two Aspects of Brother Nee's Ministry— Christ and the Church

Brother Nee's ministry was clearly of two aspects—Christ and the church. His ministry was a fully, properly, and adequately balanced ministry. Through my reading and knowledge of church history, I have come to know something concerning the lives of many famous spiritual persons from the first century to the present. I never saw a person like Brother Nee who was so adequately and thoroughly balanced with these two aspects—Christ and the church. He really saw the vision of Christ, and he also received the revelation of the church. His publications were always on Christ and the church. They were properly balanced (see pages 5 and 6 of the foreword to *The Orthodoxy of the Church* published by Living Stream Ministry). He published many books concerning Christ as life and everything to us. The reality, or the content, of the church is Christ Himself. He also published many books on the practice, the practicality, of the church. Brother Nee's ministry on Christ was not for the believers individually. The vision of Christ which Brother Nee received for his ministry was of Christ for the church.

Many so-called spiritual people teach about Christ for the Christians individually. In their teaching they do not care for the church. They are even afraid to speak about the church because they realize that this will cause problems. To stay away from these problems, they just take care of Christ for the believers' individual life. Brother Nee was different. The vision he received was concerning Christ as the believers' life and everything for the building up of the church.

The Christ whom the believers experience is the reality, the content, of the church. In order to match this reality, the practicality of the church is needed. The reality of the church is the content. The practicality of the church is the expression. Christ is not merely for the individual Christians but for the corporate Body of Christ. His being for the individual Christians is for the building up of His corporate Body.

The church's reality is Christ being realized by us individual Christians in a corporate way. To match this reality, we need the practice of the church. We cannot hold Christ as the reality in an individual way. We must come out of our private interests and come together with Christ as the reality to practice the church life. Then we can testify, even to God's enemy, that we are one and that we have not only the reality but also the practicality of the church.

Christ and the church were the main points of Brother Nee's ministry. I have realized what Brother Nee's ministry is to such an extent by reading his books and by being with him. I thank God and praise the Lord that I had the privilege of listening to his messages, of having personal, direct talks with him, and of seeing how he conducted himself. When I initially read some of his articles in 1925, I thought he must be an old, experienced man. Eventually, I found out that he was a very young man. At that time he was twenty-two years old and I was twenty. I first came into contact with him by reading his publications.

Eventually, I read all of Brother Nee's writings. I also edited many of his messages. I was assigned to edit one of his three series of editions of *The Christian*. Beginning in 1934 the main messages in that magazine were from Brother Nee, but I did the editing. Thus, I had the privilege of reading all these writings. His writings show that his ministry was of two aspects—Christ and the church. Christ is the reality, the content, of the church, and the church needs the practicality to match the reality.

In 1923 Brother Nee published his first magazine called *The Present Testimony*. His second magazine, *The Christian*, began to be published in 1925 and continued for two years through 1926. After 1926 Brother Nee began to publish *The Present Testimony* again for about seven years. *The Present Testimony* was mainly on the side of Christ being life to us. It presented the revelation of the person and work of Christ, the death of Christ, the resurrection of Christ, and the ascension of Christ. That was the deepest spiritual publication in all of Christianity at that time. *The Christian* mainly covered things for young Christians, for new beginners. In 1934 Brother Nee had the burden to publish *The Christian* again. By that time I was in the work, so he gave the editing responsibility to me. From that year he took care of *The Present Testimony*, and I was charged to take care of *The Christian*. Besides this he published many books on both Christ and the church. His ministry was composed of Christ and the church.

The Acceptance of Brother Nee's Ministry on Christ but the Rejection of His Ministry on the Practicality of the Church

Many in Christianity accept Brother Nee's ministry on Christ, but they reject his ministry on the practicality of the church. I have shared previously how Brother Nee went to visit the Plymouth Brethren in England in 1933. Before that time he had read many of the Brethren's writings. Also, through Miss M. E. Barber, he became acquainted with the writings of Jesse Penn-Lewis and T. Austin-Sparks. When he went to visit the Brethren in 1933, he also went to visit Brother Austin-Sparks at Honor Oak in London. The Brethren were bothered about this because they were exclusive. They thought that Brother Nee had joined them and that he should not contact Brother Austin-Sparks' group. During that time the Brethren took him to Canada and the United States. When he returned, he personally told me all the things concerning his trip.

In our consideration we realized that we could neither follow the way of the Brethren nor follow the way of Brother Austin-Sparks. The way of the Brethren was exclusive, and the way of Brother Austin-Sparks was without practicality. The Brethren wrote us several letters, and we replied to them in 1935.

Later Brother Nee went to Europe again in 1938, and he stayed there for one and a half years to have more fellowship. Mostly he was with Brother Austin-Sparks' group at Honor

Oak. He was also invited to speak in some of the Scandinavian countries. In those one and a half years, he ministered mainly on the aspect of Christ as life because he realized that the people there were not ready to accept the aspect of the church in a practical way. *The Normal Christian Life* is a collection of the messages Brother Nee gave then. These messages were collected and edited by Angus Kinnear, who was a medical student under Brother Nee's teaching.

While Brother Nee was there, he also translated *The Normal Christian Church Life* from Chinese to English. He did that, of course, with a purpose. This book was translated in London while he was staying at Honor Oak. Miss Fishbacher helped him in this translation work. That book was printed by the bookroom of Brother Austin-Sparks. After it was published, it stirred up some problems. Brother Austin-Sparks told me many years later that *The Normal Christian Church Life* should either not be published anymore or that some corrections and changes should be made in it. Of course, *The Normal Christian Church Life* is about the practicality of the church and the truth concerning one church in one city.

At the end of Brother Nee's one-and-a-half-year stay in England, the people at Honor Oak had a farewell meeting for him and asked him to give a word. He gave a short word saying that people's talking about the church is like carpenters' talking about making a chair. It is one thing to talk about making a chair, but where is the chair? Then he said, "Many people are talking about the church, but I would ask, 'Where is the church?'"

Brother Nee was at Honor Oak in 1938. Twenty years later I was invited to the same place by Brother Austin-Sparks. I stayed there for one month in 1958. Brother Austin-Sparks turned all the meetings over to me. These included both the conference meetings and all the regular meetings. The night before I was going to leave, there was a meeting. I went to the meeting with the thought that I would not be asked to speak since I was going to leave the next day. Then Brother Austin-Sparks came to me and said, "Brother Lee, you have to speak tonight." I said that I did not have any thought about speaking. He jokingly responded by reminding me that I had said that in the church life, we had to take care of the feeling of the brothers. I took his word and went to the platform, without any thought beforehand about what I should speak. When I was on the platform, I asked the congregation to read Revelation 1. Then I shared that the ministry is for the local churches, not the local churches for the ministry. Regardless of how good, how spiritual, and how high one's ministry is, it still must be for the local churches. Regardless of how degraded the local churches are, they are still the lampstands.

Eventually, I found out that Brother Austin-Sparks' way was the opposite of this. His way was to use a group of believers to support his ministry. That meant that his meeting was for the ministry, and the ministry was not for the church. A few years after I gave that final message at Honor Oak, someone told me that my word tore down the whole situation there. The entire month that I was there, Brother Austin-Sparks was always with me on the platform, presiding over the meetings. After the meetings were over, he was always so happy with me because I was speaking concerning Christ as life, just as he did. But after I gave that final message, he quickly walked down from the platform by himself, leaving me there alone. As I walked down from the platform by myself, one of the elders there came to me and said that Brother Nee's ministry concerning the church and its practicality had been rejected there twenty years ago. He said that the Lord had not forgotten this and sent me there twenty years later to remind them of the same thing.

In 1938 and 1939, Brother Nee was fully accepted by the seeking Christians in northern Europe in his ministry on Christ as life. But on the practicality of the church, the spiritual situation in that area did not allow him to fulfill his ministry completely. When he came back to China after this time, he had his first conference on the Body of Christ. He cabled me, asking me to come to Shanghai for that conference. During that time he told me the stories about his time in Europe. He told me that on the whole earth, there was only one group that could "echo" what we had seen of the Body of Christ. That was Brother Austin-Sparks' group. Brother Nee, however, said that there was a big "but." They saw something concerning the principle of the Body, but they did not see the practical side of the church life. Brother Nee told me and another brother much concerning his time at Honor Oak. The other brother proposed that we invite Brother Austin-Sparks to come to us. Brother Nee was really wise. He said that the time was not ripe.

Eventually, I was sent from mainland China to Taiwan, and we started the work there in 1949. After six years, in 1955, there was a great increase in our number. Some of the leading ones in Taiwan received some letters from abroad encouraging them to invite Brother Austin-Sparks. Two of the leading ones in Taiwan thought we needed the help in spirituality. I agreed with them, but I said that we had to be careful. I told the brothers that in a recent issue of Brother Austin-Sparks' paper, *The Witness and the Testimony*, there was a small paragraph written by him in which he expressed his thanks to the people who sent him Christmas cards. That was the January issue of 1955. I told the brothers that we had been enlightened by the Lord to cast down and give up all the things related to Christmas. Yet here was a spiritual person still expressing his thanks to the people who gave him Christmas cards. I told them that we know people not always by the main points but by the small things. This is because people can be very careful about the main points. They can pretend and cover things. But they are careless with the small things. We have to learn to know people not by the "head" but by the "tail."

For this reason I told the brothers that we had to be careful. We had good fellowship with those Christians in England. But I said, "Suppose we invite him to come and he is dissenting in something. Then we will have trouble. It might be better to keep our good fellowship with him without any direct contact." Two weeks later the two brothers again brought up the subject of inviting Brother Austin-Sparks. I went along with them, agreeing to invite him. I wrote the invitation, and he came to Taiwan in 1955.

Our time with him was wonderful during his first visit.

He ministered on the spiritual side of Christ as life according to what we expected. Then we invited him to come a second time, but during his second visit he opposed the practicality of the church, the ground of the church. I had over thirty long talks with him. Each session was about two or three hours. But he was greatly opposed to the ground of the church. The practicality of the church is a great truth, but to practice this truth requires the paying of a price.

I say again that Brother Nee's ministry in the aspect of Christ was fully accepted, but his ministry in the aspect of the church was fully rejected. Some may feel that it is sufficient just to publish Brother Nee's books concerning Christ. However, it is altogether unfair to hide the books by Brother Nee concerning the church. This is dishonest. I was with Brother Nee day after day for many years, and he opened up his heart to me many times. I can say, at the very least, that I was one of three persons who knew him to the uttermost. I know where he stood. I was sent out of mainland China by Brother Nee. I asked him why he made such a decision. He told me that maybe the enemy would wipe us out in China. He said that if I were to go out, we would still have something left. In this sense, I was charged by him to be responsible for what the Lord had shown to him. The more that people try to hide Brother Nee's books on the church, the more burdened I am to put them out.

Eventually, a false rumor of two aspects was being spread. The first aspect was that Brother Nee changed his concept about the practicality of the church, the ground of the church, after the Second World War. The second aspect was that because Witness Lee is so much for the practicality of the church life, he is different from Watchman Nee. There is still a struggle and a battle concerning the practicality of the church life. When we published *Further Talks on the Church Life*, I documented every chapter. At the beginning of each chapter are the date and the place where the message was given. This proves that after the war, Brother Nee did not change his concept about the practice of the church. All of the messages in *Further Talks on the Church Life* were given by Brother Nee from 1948 to 1951. In these messages Brother

Nee confirmed that what he had seen in 1937 concerning the practicality of the church life was absolutely right. He had not changed at all in his view concerning the ground of the church.

It is absolutely dishonest to give people a wrong impression that Brother Nee was only for the revelation and experience of Christ and not for the church life. I have the burden to put out all of his books on the practicality of the church life. There has been a real struggle and battle over this truth and its practice. I have been suffering for many years because of this one thing. Because of Brother Austin-Sparks' dissenting speaking in the Far East, some young people were influenced and became rebellious. They held the concept that there was no need to have a practical church life. They felt that as long as we live by Christ, we are spiritually the Body of Christ.

The battle is still raging today over the revelation and ministry of Brother Nee, which was concerning both Christ and the church. To publish merely the books by him concerning Christ, in a sense, is a help to the saints. But in another sense, it is a cheating and a deceiving. This is not fair to Brother Nee. If people are fair, they should put out all the writings by Brother Nee and let the readers have their own discernment. We all have to be clear about how subtle the enemy is. I am happy to see Brother Nee's books on Christ as life published, but it is the enemy's subtlety that the books by Brother Nee on the practicality of the church life would be hidden. It is also a devilish, subtle lie to say that Brother Nee changed his concept concerning the church and that because of this, Witness Lee is different from Watchman Nee.

It is because of the practicality of the church that I am suffering so much opposition and so many attacks. But what can I do? I have to be faithful to the Lord, and I also have to be loyal to Brother Nee's commission. We have to realize that in all the battles and struggles, the victory is the Lord's. He has won the victory. We need to see where we are standing today and the real ministry which the Lord has given us through Brother Nee. His ministry was not the ministry of

Christ only. His ministry was the ministry of Christ for the church. Christ and the church—this is our vision, this is what we are suffering for, and eventually this becomes our ministry.

CHAPTER NINE

THE HISTORY OF THE LOCAL CHURCHES

(7)

Scripture Reading: Gal. 1:4, 13-16; 5:11; Rev. 2:6, 9, 14-15, 20, 24; 3:7-9, 20; 17:4-5; 18:4

THE REVELATIONS, THE SUFFERINGS, THE MINISTRY, THE WORK, AND THE CHURCHES

Thus far in our fellowship, we have covered five main categories of items related to the history of the local churches: the revelations, the sufferings, the ministry, the work, and the churches. We saw that from the revelations plus the sufferings comes the ministry. With the ministry, we have the work which produces the churches. The work comes not out of certain doctrines, gifts, or practices, but out of the ministry. The ministry is composed, produced, and formed through revelations mingled with sufferings. This corresponds with the experience of the apostle Paul. First, he received revelations from the Lord. In addition to receiving these revelations, Paul passed through many sufferings. Out of this came the ministry. By and with the ministry, Paul worked, and that work produced the churches.

Today in this age the principle is the same. The Lord gives us the revelations. Then He puts us into a certain environment of sufferings so that we may have the ministry. With this ministry we work, and out of this work the churches are produced. The spreading of the practice of the church life comes from a work by the definite ministry, which is composed with sufferings and revelations. What the Lord has led us to pass through in His recovery is according to the record of the New Testament.

BEING RESCUED OUT OF THE PRESENT EVIL AGE

Our history is a history of being delivered from the present evil age. This is according to Paul's word in Galatians 1:4. The book of Galatians opens in a unique way. Actually, every book of the Bible opens in a specific way. Genesis opens by saying that in the beginning God created the heavens and the earth. John opens by telling us that in the beginning was the Word. First Corinthians opens by showing us that we can call on the name of the Lord to enjoy Him as our portion. Galatians, a short book of six chapters, opens with a word that cannot be found in any other book. In verse 4 Paul said that the Lord Jesus Christ "gave Himself for our sins, that He might rescue us out of the present evil age, according to the will of our God and Father." Some might expect Paul to say that Christ gave Himself for our sins so that we might be delivered from hell, but Paul did not say this. Paul said that Christ died for our sins so that He might rescue us out of the present evil age. This is according to the will of our God and Father.

The book of Ephesians reveals that the will of God is to have the church as a living Body for Christ (1:22-23; 3:10-11). It is not to have an organization but an organism. The will of God is not to have the Jewish religion or the religion of Christianity. The will of God is to have the organic Body of Christ. It is not to have circumcision or uncircumcision. The will of God is to have a new creation (Gal. 6:15). The new creation is the new man (Col. 3:10), and this new man is the church.

Christ gave Himself for our sins to deliver us out of the present evil age according to the will of God. We need to see the difference between the age and the world. In Ephesians 2:2 Paul said that we once walked according to the age of this world. The world refers to the satanic system composed of many ages. An age is a part, a section, an aspect, the present and modern appearance, of the system of Satan, which is used by him to usurp and occupy people and keep them away from God and His purpose. The world is the whole system, and in this system there are different ages. Satan has formed this anti-God world system to systematize men with religion, culture, education, industry, commerce, entertainment, etc., through men's fallen nature in their lusts, pleasures, pursuits, and even in their indulgence in living necessities, such as food, clothing, housing, and transportation. The whole of such a satanic system lies in the evil one (1 John 5:19).

The present evil age at Paul's time was Judaism, the prevailing Jewish religion. Paul continues his thought about this evil age in Galatians 1:13 and 14 by telling us how he was in that age: "For you have heard of my manner of life formerly in Judaism, that I persecuted the church of God excessively and ravaged it; and I advanced in Judaism beyond many contemporaries in my race, being more exceedingly zealous of the traditions of my fathers." This describes how Paul was in that religious section of the satanic system.

What is Satan's aim? His aim is to systematize people into his world and keep them away from God's will to have the Body of Christ. As long as we are kept away from the Body of Christ, we are kept away from the will of God and are systematized into Satan's system. Satan uses worldly entertainment, sinful things, and even religious things to systematize people away from God's will. In Paul's day, Satan used Judaism to systematize all the Pharisees, scribes, priests, and elders among the Jewish people. Today Satan uses the religion of Christianity to systematize many of the Lord's people away from God's will to have the organic Body of Christ.

Romans 12:2 says, "And do not be conformed to this age, but be transformed by the renewing of the mind, that you may prove by testing what the will of God is, that which is good and well-pleasing and perfect." The will of God is the Body life. We need to get into the Body life. As long as we are outside of the Body life, we are outside of God's will. The main prevailing thing that keeps us away from God's will, the Body of Christ, is the age. Therefore, we should not be conformed to this age. Religion, in Paul's eyes according to Galatians, was an age, a section of Satan's system. We should not be conformed to any religion. Paul said that he had been delivered out of that. In the past, he had been in Judaism, advancing in Judaism beyond all his peers. He was a top religionist, but one day the Lord appeared to him and gained him. From that time Paul did not preach Judaism. He preached Christ, the living factor to produce all the churches.

Second Timothy and Revelation show that at the end of Paul's life and John's life, the churches had become degraded. Eventually, the degradation continued to such an extent that another religious system developed. Paul was delivered out of the age of Judaism. Today the real Christians and seekers of Christ have to be delivered out of the religious system of Christianity. The Lord's people have to hear His call: "Come out of her, My people..." (Rev. 18:4). This is the call to come out of Babylon, the religious system of Christianity.

One of the most damaging items in Christianity is the clergy-laity system. In Revelation 2:6 the Lord said, "But this you have, that you hate the works of the Nicolaitans, which I also hate." The root word for *Nicolaitan* in Greek is composed of two words—*niko* and *laos*. *Niko* means *conquer* or *above others*, and *laos* means *laity*. The Nicolaitans must have been a group of people who esteemed themselves to be higher than the common believers. They formed a clergy to rule over and conquer the people with the excuse that the people were mere laymen who did not know the Bible.

The Nicolaitans are the so-called experts, the clergy who form a hierarchy. This system has been adopted by the Roman Catholic Church and has also been retained by the Protestant churches. Today in the Roman Catholic Church there is the priestly system, in the state churches there is the clerical system, and in the independent churches there is the pastoral system. Many pastors are even designated with the title *Reverend*, to show that they are in this special class of clergy.

Revelation 2:6 speaks of the works of the Nicolaitans, and 2:15 speaks of the teaching of the Nicolaitans. This clergy-laity system caused the church to become the religious system of Christianity, which is another religious age. Paul needed to be delivered from Judaism, the religious age at his time. Today we need to be delivered from Christianity, the religious age in our time.

I am sharing this to help us realize that the history among us has been one of coming completely out of Christianity without compromise. It is a shame that some so-called co-workers among us have tried their best to compromise. They say that between the denominations and the local churches there is a gap, and they consider themselves as the bridge to bridge the gap. This was a suffering to Brother Nee, and today this is a suffering to me.

Since 1927, just two years after I was saved, I began to be delivered out of the present evil age, the age of Christianity. Some have told me that I should not say that Christianity is degraded. But according to Revelation 17, the religious system of Christianity is a great prostitute. Verse 5 calls this great prostitute "Babylon the Great, The Mother of the Prostitutes." We need to be delivered from this mother and from her daughters, who are the prostitutes. Since the Mother of the Prostitutes is the apostate Roman Catholic Church, the prostitutes, her daughters, should be all the different sects and groups in Christianity who hold to some extent the teaching, practices, and traditions of the apostate Roman Church. We need to be delivered out of this present evil age. We have to come out of Christianity and come back to the Body of Christ. The pure church life has no evil transmitted from the apostate church.

Because of our standing for the pure church life, others have been offended. But what can we do? Paul said in Galatians 1:10, "If I were still pleasing men, I would not be a slave of Christ." If we were men-pleasers, we would not suffer persecution as Paul did. The history of the Lord's recovery is a history of coming out of and being outside of the present evil age. We have burned the bridges between us and Christianity, but some among us have tried to build a bridge to bring us back. We need to burn all the bridges. There should be no bridge between the local churches and Christianity. Everything should be after its kind. The denominations are after their kind, and the local churches should be after their kind. We should be what we are without compromise or pretense.

I am afraid that in the coming years, if the Lord delays His coming, some subtle ones will be used by the enemy again to try to bridge the gap between us and Christianity. We need to maintain such a gap between us and Christianity.

The wider this gap is the better because it is a gap between us and the present evil age. Thank the Lord that Brother Nee was a pioneer ahead of us to come out of Christianity into the pure church life to accomplish God's will to have the Body of Christ. He suffered for this his entire life. He was even imprisoned by the Communists for the last twenty years of his life. There was a rumor saying that he was released, but this is a lie. He died in prison in his faithfulness to the Lord. There was no change with him. He was a real martyr. He was martyred for the church and the churches. He was really delivered from this present evil age.

Many of those who praise Brother Nee today would actually oppose him if he were here. The scribes and Pharisees excused themselves by saying that if they had been in the days of the prophets, they would not have participated in the deeds of their fathers, who murdered the prophets. The Lord Jesus exposed them by saying that although they built the graves of the prophets, they were witnesses to themselves that they were the sons of those who murdered the prophets (Matt. 23:29-31). Then He went on to say that, in the same way, they would kill and persecute the prophets sent to them (vv. 34-35). Brother Nee was persecuted and opposed because he came out of the present evil age to accomplish God's will to have the organic Body of Christ. Our history is a history outside of the present evil age.

THE FOUR MAIN REVIVALS AMONG US

Now I would like to share something concerning the four main revivals among us. We have seen that the revelations plus the sufferings produce the ministry. By the ministry we have the work, and out of the work comes the churches. In addition to this, even in the Lord's recovery, we need periodic revivals. In the Lord's recovery in China, there were clearly and definitely four big revivals.

The Revival concerning
the Assurance of Salvation

The first revival in China was related to the recovery of the truth concerning the assurance of salvation. Robert

Morrison was the first Protestant missionary to China in the early 1800s. From that time until Brother Nee was caught by the Lord in 1920, the assurance of salvation had not been made clear. The Lord gave Brother Nee a clear vision of the assurance of salvation. Brother Nee told people that as long as they believed in the Lord Jesus according to the teaching and revelation of the Bible, they could have the assurance that they were saved. Many were revived by his messages on the assurance of salvation. Brother Nee's preaching issued in a revival in 1923 in his hometown, Foochow.

In those early days of the Lord's move in China, Brother Nee fasted and prayed every Saturday for the entire day. He told me personally that he would abstain from eating the whole day and pray for the entire day in preparation for his speaking the next day. For about a year, he fasted and prayed on Saturday and preached on the Lord's Day. During that time nearly all his classmates were saved. The entire atmosphere of his school changed. Everywhere at the school, students could be seen reading the Bible, praying together, or fellowshipping together.

During this time of revival, Brother Nee and some other young brothers with him heard that in Nanking, far away from their hometown, a young Christian had been raised up by the Lord named Ruth Lee. She was the editor of a very famous and prevailing Christian paper called *The Spiritual Light*. Brother Nee and the brothers invited her to come to their hometown to hold some meetings. She agreed to come and would make the trip by boat. Brother Nee realized that as a sister, she should not be put to the forefront too much, even though he and the other brothers were much younger than she was. He thought that he would let the others go to the pier to meet her and that he would not go.

That night Brother Nee had a dream. In Acts 2 on the day of Pentecost, Peter indicated that when the Spirit is poured out upon people, they will dream dreams (v. 17). Brother Nee personally told me about his dream, just as he related all the history from 1920 to 1932 to me. In this dream he and others were going to welcome Sister Lee, and the boat came. While he was standing there at a distance, he saw a young lady walking from the boat toward the people welcoming her. Then the Lord told him, "This is the co-worker I have prepared for you."

When he awoke in the morning, he considered that this could have been a dream from the Lord, so he had better go to meet her. He went with a hesitant attitude, wondering whether or not his dream was of the Lord. Instead of going to the front, he stood at the rear. He saw the young people running to the boat to welcome Sister Lee. He had no idea what she looked like before that time, but she was the exact person he had seen in his dream. When they brought Miss Lee to him, he said, "I saw her already." But the others did not know that he meant that he had seen her already in a dream the previous night. He did not relate his dream to Miss Lee until about four years later in 1927. The Lord arranged an environment in which she was forced to give up her work in Nanking. Then she came to Shanghai, and from that time she worked with Brother Nee.

The meetings which Brother Nee held in Foochow when Miss Lee came brought in a big revival. Because the saints there did not have a big hall, they eventually met in an open field. Everyone in the congregation brought a chair with him. If someone did not bring a chair, he had to stand. Many were saved during this time, and that was the first revival among us. The news of this revival spread to many places, and many were helped to become clear about the assurance of salvation.

The Revival concerning
the Overcoming Life of Christ

The second revival among us happened twelve years later in 1935. By that time many churches had been raised up, but we had become somewhat cold. Brother Nee himself also had the feeling that he needed some burning. Thus, he made the decision in the spring of 1935 to go to England. He also decided that before going, he would come to my hometown of Chefoo.

Brother Nee and his wife stayed in my home. While he was staying there, we had a conference for one week. In that conference he ministered day after day on the overcoming life of Christ. Through this prevailing conference, we were all revived. We were all on fire again. He canceled his trip to Europe and returned to Shanghai to hold another conference. The fire of that revival burned the church in Shanghai in 1935.

This was the second revival among us which helped us to experience the overcoming life of Christ. Before that time we came to know the life of Christ, and we had some experience of the death of Christ, but what we had come to know and experience was not that prevailing. Through that revival we were brought into a full realization and a rich experience of the overcoming life of Christ.

The Revival concerning the Practicality of the Church Life

The third revival among us was in 1942 and 1943. First, we were revived with the truth concerning the assurance of salvation. Second, we were set on fire with the overcoming life of Christ. The third revival was with the practicality of the church life. That revival transpired again in my hometown of Chefoo.

Before that revival, Brother Nee had a big turn in 1939. In that year he saw the Body of Christ and the practicality of the local church. I went in 1939 to attend his conference on the Body of Christ. Then I went to his training in 1940. At that time I received much help from him, mainly from the private talks he had with me. Through those talks I saw what he called the blueprint of the practicality of the local church.

Later I returned to Chefoo in northern China. Once I returned, I did not have the liberty to move anymore because of the war. I realized that it was the Lord's will for me not to travel but to stay in Chefoo to practice the church life in a practical way. From January 1941 we practiced everything that I had seen in Shanghai from Brother Nee. We had the proper eldership, the deacons, the service office, and the service groups. We practiced the church life for two years according to the blueprint Brother Nee had seen. At the end of 1942 the church in Chefoo experienced a great revival.

This revival came through the practicality of the church life with all the service groups. The practicality of the church life brought all the saints into the building. The church in Chefoo had about eight hundred saints at that time.

By January 1, 1943 the revival in Chefoo was at its peak. No announcements were made beforehand to have a meeting on that day, but the saints came and met. From morning to evening, everyone met together without eating or drinking. There was no schedule or program, but many things were carried out by the Lord that day. After a couple of weeks, our meetings were similar to those recorded in Acts 2 and 4. We met day after day for over one hundred days. That was a one-hundred-day conference beginning on January 1, 1943. Every meeting was different and new.

It would take many messages for me to relate all the wonderful things that happened during that period of time. I would like to relate a few things to give us some idea of what was taking place. During one afternoon, a young man, who was a student of about nineteen or twenty years of age, was reading the Bible. He read Isaiah 1:3-4, which says, "The ox knows his owner, / And the donkey, his master's manger; / But Israel does not know, / My people do not much consider. / Alas, sinful nation, / A people heavy with iniquity, / Seed of evildoers, / Children acting corruptly! / They have forsaken Jehovah; / They have despised the Holy One of Israel; / They have become estranged and have gone backward." He also read Jeremiah 8:7, which says, "Yea, the stork in the heavens knoweth her appointed times; and the turtledove and the swallow and the crane observe the time of their coming; but my people know not the law of Jehovah" (ASV). He was very inspired by these verses.

The Lord impressed him within that he should stand up that evening in the meeting to give a testimony concerning these two portions of the Word. He was very fearful of doing this since he was very timid. He told the Lord, "If you want me to give a testimony tonight, you have to do one thing. You have to ask Brother Lee to stand up to read these two portions of the Word to all the people." I had never talked to him before, and I did not even know his name. He thought it would be impossible for me to do this, but he told the Lord that he would not give a testimony unless this happened. At a certain point in the meeting, we all knelt down to pray. While we were praying, the Lord told me within to ask the saints to rise up and read Isaiah 1:3-4. He was amazed. Then I said, "Turn to Jeremiah 8:7." He was trembling. After we read this verse, he gave a testimony, sharing with us about how the Lord had dealt with him concerning these verses. This is one illustration of the prevailing move of the Spirit at that time.

The move of the Spirit was also prevailing in all the homes of the saints. The saints offered all of their possessions to the church. Every evening all kinds of offerings were given to the church. Just to keep an account of those offerings took much time. Everyone came to the meeting with something to offer, so we had to have different groups to keep an account of the different kinds of offerings. One group, for example, kept a record of all the title deeds to property that were offered. All those who owned any kind of property brought their title deeds and offered them to the church. By the last day of this revival, everyone literally offered all the things they had. Even things such as typewriters and sewing machines were offered.

Eventually, seventy saints traveled by boat from Chefoo to inner Mongolia, migrating there for the spread of the church life. They offered all that they had to the church, and the church assigned a certain amount of money and material things to each of them, which was enough for them to travel and live on for three months. Our experience in those days was just like the beginning of the church life when "those who believed were together and had all things common; and they sold their possessions and properties and divided them among all according as anyone had need" (Acts 2:44-45).

In my whole Christian life, I have never seen a revival like that. In all the homes, there was not any loose talk or gossip. All that the saints spoke was Christ, the church, and the Lord's migration. Every home—old and young, fathers, mothers, and children—was stirred up without one exception. At that time we called ourselves "the host, the army, of

Jehovah." Such a situation was the result of our being in the practicality of the church life. The saints entered into the service groups in the church life, and this caused them to be burned. Then the revival came in. During that revival many young people were raised up who later became leading ones in the churches.

The Biggest, Most Powerful, and Most Prevailing Revival among Us through the Recovery of Brother Nee's Ministry

After the war I was invited to come to Shanghai. I was still on the peak of the revival in Chefoo, so that revival was brought to Shanghai. This was the fourth main revival among us.

We have seen how Brother Nee was unable to minister for six years, from 1942 to 1948, because of the rebellious turmoil in Shanghai. Through the revival there in 1947 and the first few months of 1948, the rebellious and dissenting ones were brought back. Nearly all of them repented and confessed to Brother Nee. That brought Brother Nee back to the ministry. Some said that Brother Nee had no time to minister from 1942 to 1948 because of his business, but this was not true. He had the time, but he did not minster because of the saints' rebellion against him. He told me this in a definite way. In 1947 I begged him to minister in Shanghai, but he said that he could not minister because of the rebellious ones there.

Thank the Lord that through the revival in 1947 the whole church in Shanghai was brought back, and eventually Brother Nee's ministry was recovered. The recovery of his ministry confirmed and enlarged the revival in the church. Later, about eighty seeking ones from different parts of China who had come to Shanghai to participate in that revival were with Brother Nee for a six-month training. After that training from April to October in 1948, the trainees returned to their localities, and their localities were set on fire. That became the biggest, most powerful, and most prevailing revival among us. This revival spread throughout all of China. In one locality, over seven hundred people were baptized in one day. Eventually, however, the Communists came to take over all of China.

The revival among us in Chefoo in 1943 spread to Shanghai in 1947. After I was sent to the island of Taiwan, this kind of revival was brought there. This was one of the reasons why the work in Taiwan went so fast in the first few years. Within six years we increased from about five hundred saints to about twenty thousand. This was due to the spreading of the flow of that big revival in China.

The main spiritual aspect of the fourth revival was that all the saints consecrated all that they were and all that they had to the church. That was not only a revival with the practicality of the church life but also a revival with the full surrender of the saints to the Lord for the church. Whatever they were, whatever they did, and whatever they possessed were handed over to the church. This uprooted all the worldly things and built all the saints together. The saints became a prevailing expression of the Body of Christ with the power and impact of the one accord. That was the practicality of the saints being built up.

Even today we are still inheriting all the good points of those four revivals. We are inheriting the experience of the assurance of salvation, the overcoming life of Christ, the practicality of the church life, and the practice of fully surrendering ourselves to the Lord for the church. I hope that we would be so clear about these four aspects: the assurance of salvation, the overcoming life of Christ, the practicality of the church life, and the full surrender of whatever we are, whatever we have, and whatever we can do, to the church.

MY REALIZATION OF BROTHER NEE
THROUGH MY CONTACT WITH HIM

At this point I would like to fellowship about my realization of Brother Nee through my contact with him. Brother Nee and I were far away from one another when we were young Christians. He was in southern China, and I was in northern China. He was saved in 1920, and I was saved in 1925. My mother was baptized as a teenager, and she became a member of a Southern Baptist denomination. I was brought up and educated in Christianity, but I was not saved. One day I heard that a young lady preacher around twenty-five years old was coming to my town to hold some gospel meetings. I was nineteen years old at that time. I was curious to see such a young woman preach the gospel.

One afternoon I went to hear her speak. Since that time I have never seen a person preaching who was that prevailing. She was preaching to a crowd of over one thousand people about how Satan has captured, possessed, and occupied people. She used the story of Pharaoh having the children of Israel under his tyranny. I was captured by the Lord because of her preaching. That young sister's name was Peace Wang. She became the second sister who was a co-worker among us after Ruth Lee. Through her preaching I was saved in April 1925. At that time as a young man, I was very ambitious, but I was really turned to the Lord.

I loved the Lord, but I had nowhere to go for help. I tried to collect books about the Bible to help me understand it. In my hometown there was a Christian paper called The Morning Star. In that paper there was an article by Brother Nee. It was the best article in the paper to me, and I enjoyed reading it. I did my best to collect all of the issues with his articles. I had never met him, and from reading his articles I thought that he must have been an old writer. In one of the issues, there was an advertisement for people who wanted to subscribe to Brother Nee's monthly magazine entitled *The Christian*. I sent in my subscription and received the twenty-four issues of *The Christian* in 1925 and 1926.

During that time I wrote to Brother Nee. This was the beginning of my contact with him through written correspondence. Mostly, I asked him questions about the Bible. In one letter I asked him to tell me the best book to help me understand the whole Bible. He told me that according to his knowledge, the best book to help me know the whole Bible was J. N. Darby's *Synopsis of the Books of the Bible*. He said that I would have to read it a number of times in order to understand it. Later when I went to visit him for the first time, he gave me a set of Darby's five-volume synopsis.

By reading Brother Nee's writings, I began to realize the truth concerning what the proper church is and the wrong-doings of Christianity. Although I was then in a denomination, I was inwardly through with the denominations. In my denomination there was a young man who noticed that I had become different from the others. One day he came to me and asked me how we could know that we are saved. I gave him a booklet by Brother Nee on the assurance of salvation. After reading that, he was clear that he was saved. Eventually, our pastor referred to us two as Joshua and Caleb.

Later this young brother was being transferred by his company from Chefoo to Shanghai. He asked me where he should meet in Shanghai. I told him that the booklet I had given him on the assurance of salvation had something in it concerning where a meeting of Christians was. I told him that he had better go there. He went to that meeting of the church in Shanghai. Eventually, he became one of the first three elders in Shanghai.

At the end of 1927, my denomination elected me to be one of the board members. By that time I was forced to tell them that I could not stay in that denomination anymore. That was the year I left them to go to a Brethren assembly. I went to Brethren assembly meetings faithfully every week. I picked up many good teachings there concerning typology and prophecy. Years later in August 1931, the Lord impressed me that I had received so much biblical knowledge, yet I was cold and dead. There was a real repentance within me. Thank the Lord that after I was saved, I never went back to the world. But by that time, although I attended so many Brethren meetings each week, I was cold.

When the Lord convicted me concerning my coldness, I rose early the next day. My home was at the foothill of a small mountain. I went to the top of this mountain and wept before the Lord with repentance. I was desperate. From that day I went there each morning to have a time with the Lord. I continued to pray in this way for a few months. During that time when I was seeking the Lord, Brother Nee held a victory conference in Shanghai in 1931. I attempted to go to Shanghai to this conference, but Japan had invaded Manchuria, and I was advised not to go. If I went, I ran the risk of being cut off from my home, so I canceled my trip. The young brother in my denomination who had gone to Shanghai returned to Chefoo the next year, and he told me about all the good meetings there.

He and I went to our former denomination, and we proposed that they should invite Brother Nee to come to speak to them. Although we had left that denomination, we left them with a very good impression of us. They still appreciated us as young men. They agreed to our proposal and invited Brother Nee. At the same time, the Southern Baptist seminary in a county close to Chefoo also invited him to speak to them.

In the summer of 1932, Brother Nee came to Chefoo, and I joined those who went to his boat to greet him. I attended all the meetings in which he spoke. I went with him to the Southern Baptist seminary, which by that time had become involved with the Pentecostal movement. In those years the Pentecostal movement was prevailing in northern China. This was the first time I had seen the practice of the Pentecostals. In the meeting some were jumping, others were rolling on the floor, some were laughing, and others were shouting. This went on for a time. Then the pastor called the meeting to order, and Brother Nee spoke. After the meeting, Brother Nee and I walked together. I remarked to him about the strange practices in their meeting. He said to me, "In the New Testament, there are no forms." Later he stayed in my home for two or three days. During this time we had long periods of fellowship. That was in July 1932.

On the evening of the day that Brother Nee left, a brother who was a member of my former denomination came to me. He was seeking help from Brother Nee, but Brother Nee had left. He and I had a long fellowship that evening at the seashore, since my home was not far away from the beach. At a certain point he said, "You have to baptize me tonight in the sea." I said that I was not a pastor, an elder, or a deacon. He rebuked me by saying, "You told me that all the disciples of Jesus, who are qualified to preach the gospel, are also qualified to baptize people. You have to baptize me." I asked him to pray with me. Then the word in Acts 8 came to me: "Look, water! What prevents me from being baptized" (v. 36). Then I baptized him. When we came up out of the water, we were both in the heavenlies. He told me that from tomorrow he would never go back to the denominations, but would come to meet with me. I told him that from tomorrow I would stop going to the Brethren meetings and would begin to meet with him. That was really the Lord's move.

His baptism took place on a Tuesday. On Thursday of the same week, another two came to us, asking us to baptize them, and we did. On the Lord's Day, more were baptized. The following Lord's Day, we had eleven brothers taking the Lord's table. That was the beginning of the first local church in north China in my hometown of Chefoo. The news of this reached Brother Nee in Shanghai. By the end of the year, there were about eighty of us meeting together.

At the beginning of the following year, there were about one hundred meeting in Chefoo. In April of that year, Sister Peace Wang came to visit us. She was the one through whom I was saved. By this time in 1933, she had become one of the prevailing co-workers. Then Brother Nee came, and he stayed with us for about ten days. Afterwards, he went to England to visit the Brethren.

During the first three weeks of August 1933, I was struggling with the Lord concerning giving up my job and serving Him full-time. The Lord was calling me inwardly to serve Him in this way. At that time my younger brother and I had the highest paying jobs among those in the church, so many of the church's needs were secretly taken care of by us. The Lord was calling me to give up my job, but I was considering what would happen if I did this. I was helping to meet the church's needs, but if I went full-time, others would have to meet my needs.

Actually, from the first day that I was saved through Sister Wang's preaching, I was called by the Lord to serve Him full-time. I knew that my destiny for my entire life was to serve the Lord in a full way. From August 1 to August 21, 1933, I was struggling with the Lord concerning this matter. On Wednesday, August 21, I fellowshipped with two of the leading ones after the prayer meeting. I explained the situation to them and asked them to pray for me that night. I could not go on another day without a definite decision in this matter. Late that night I had a time with the Lord, and it was so clear that His will was for me to answer His call. The only thing causing me to hesitate was my unbelief. Then the Lord impressed me that if I did not answer His call, He would be through with me as far as His work was concerned. I told the Lord with tears that I would answer His call and take His way.

The next day I resigned from my job. After resigning I went to the post office the following day to pick up a letter there for me from Manchuria. This was the first letter which I received inviting me to come to a place to speak for the Lord. I accepted this invitation and went to the capital of Manchuria to speak for the Lord's interest. While I was there, a letter came to me from my general manager, saying that he did not want me to leave my job. He said he would promote me and increase my monthly pay if I would stay. Usually at the end of the year, the employees of this company received a good bonus. I considered that if I worked for another three months, I would receive this bonus, and then I could drop my job.

When I returned home from Manchuria, there was a letter awaiting me from Brother Nee. It was a short note from him dated August 17. This was within the three-week period of time in which I was struggling with the Lord. This note said, "Brother Witness, concerning your future—I feel that you have to serve the Lord full-time. How do you feel about this? May the Lord lead you." That short note still means so much to me. That annulled the letter from my general manager. I told the Lord that even if my company offered me the whole world, I would not take it. Then I made the decision to go to Shanghai to see Brother Nee.

When I went to Shanghai, I asked Brother Nee why he wrote that note on August 17. He said that at that time his boat was on the Mediterranean while he was returning from Europe to China. When he was in his cabin, he had a burden to pray for the work in China. While he was praying, the Lord said to him within, "You have to write a note to Witness Lee telling him that you feel he should serve the Lord full-time." While Brother Nee was sailing on the Mediterranean, I was struggling with the Lord in China. We were a thousand miles apart, yet he received a burden from the Lord to write me this note at such a critical time. That fully convinced me that he was a real man of God. I realized that I had to work with him for the Lord's move. That was the beginning of our working together.

Chapter Ten

THE HISTORY OF THE LOCAL CHURCHES

(8)

Scripture Reading: John 17:21; Rom. 16:17; 1 Cor. 1:10, 12-13a; Titus 3:10; Eph. 2:22; 4:16; 1 Pet. 2:5; Rev. 1:11-12; 2:7; 22:17a

We have to realize that our history is not that of an organization or of a movement. It is a history of the Lord's recovery. A recovery is the restoration or return to a normal condition after degradation, damage, or loss. The Lord's recovery brings us back to the beginning to have the proper church life. In the early days of the Lord's recovery in China, the Lord showed us the wrongdoings of Christendom, on the negative side, and the church, on the positive side.

THE LORD'S RECOVERY BRINGING US
FULLY OUT OF BABYLON AND FULLY BACK
TO BEING IN THE SPIRIT AND IN THE BODY

It has been very difficult for us to fully come out of the old and unscriptural practices and concepts in Christendom. Christendom has been on earth for hundreds of years. It bears the name of Christ, it holds the Holy Scriptures, and it preaches the Lord Jesus as the Savior. These three items are positive, but Christendom is a mixture of these positive things with things other than Christ.

According to the book of Revelation, Christendom is the great prostitute and is called "Babylon the Great, The Mother of the Prostitutes and the Abominations of the Earth" (17:5). This evil woman is seen holding "a golden cup full of abominations and the unclean things of her fornication" (v. 4). In typology gold signifies something divine, something of God. This means that the apostate church has something of God in outward appearance, but within her golden cup are idolatry, pagan practices, and satanic things in a heretical, religious relationship. Christendom holds something divine, but there is a devilish element within it.

This was predicted by the Lord Jesus in Matthew 13. In this chapter the Lord said, "The kingdom of the heavens is like leaven, which a woman took and hid in three measures of meal until the whole was leavened" (v. 33). Meal for making the meal offering signifies Christ as food to both God and man. Leaven in the Scriptures signifies evil things (1 Cor. 5:6, 8) and evil doctrines (Matt. 16:6, 11-12). Fallen, degraded Christendom is a mixture of leaven with fine flour.

Christendom has a devilish element, but it still holds something divine. It holds a golden cup, but within the cup are abominations and unclean things related to spiritual fornication. The golden cup is the outward appearance, but the inward reality is abominable. It is easy for people to realize the outward appearance, but it is difficult to realize the inward reality. The appearance is divine, but the reality is devilish. Because Christendom is a mixture, when one gets the fine flour, he also gets the leaven because these two have become one. This is why it has been difficult for us to fully come out of Christendom.

Although I had contact with Brother Nee's ministry in 1925, I did not come into the Lord's recovery in a full way until 1932. Since that time I have seen the recovery passing through a process of coming out of Christendom. Even today we have not come out of Christendom in a thorough way. We still have something of Christendom within us, even unconsciously. When we come to a meeting, we may expect a good speaker to speak to us. In nature, this is the element and cause of fallen Christendom. This is the evil element of Nicolaitanism, the clergy-laity system, which the Lord hates (Rev. 2:6). Why do we not come to the meetings prepared to minister something? We may say that we are weak, but we are strong in expecting to listen to a good message. We may dislike going to a meeting where there is not a good speaker. This is the subtle element of the clergy-laity system still remaining within us.

The Lord's recovery is for bringing us out of this

unscriptural system and back to the beginning of the pure practice of the church life according to the divine revelation. In the beginning the saints were focused on the divine Spirit mingled with their human spirit—the mingled spirit (Rom. 8:16; 1 Cor. 6:17; Rom. 8:4). The saints, the chosen ones, the saved ones, were in the spirit enjoying Christ, experiencing Christ, and expressing Christ in a corporate way. That was the church life in the beginning. In this proper church life, there were no religion, no outward regulations, no rituals, and no vain doctrines or teachings. The saints were exercised to be in the spirit to enjoy Christ, to experience Christ, and to express and speak Christ in a corporate way.

Through all the years of the history of the local churches, the Lord has been recovering us little by little. The progress of this recovery has been somewhat hindered, though, because of our dullness. Today we are still somewhat under the "drugging" influence of Christendom. The Lord's recovery is to bring us up out of a fallen situation. It is easy to be down, but to be brought up is difficult. To be brought up is a struggle. The Lord in His recovery is bringing us up and up to His divine standard. The more we are brought up, the simpler we become. The more we are brought up, the more we become nothing.

In books such as Romans and Ephesians, there are many teachings, but in Revelation, there is just the spirit—the sevenfold intensified Spirit of God (1:4; 4:5; 5:6) and the human spirit (1:10; 4:2; 17:3; 21:10). John was in spirit and he saw the golden lampstands—one lampstand for one city (1:10-12). He did not see thousands of believers. He saw only one lampstand for one city. This is so simple. The many believers in a city should be just one lampstand in one accord, without disputation, different opinions, or different concepts and divisions. Thank the Lord that we are here today standing in oneness, but in our hearts we may still hold on to something of ourselves and something other than Christ. In God's eyes, a local church must be so simple. It should be a lampstand of pure gold without mixture—so simple, single, and pure.

To each of the seven churches in Revelation 2 and 3, the Lord says, "He who has an ear, let him hear what the Spirit says to the churches" (2:7, 11, 17, 29; 3:6, 13, 22). This is so simple—the Spirit speaks to the churches. Eventually, the entire Bible consummates with the Spirit and the bride (Rev. 22:17a). By God's work throughout the ages, all the saints and the Spirit speak the same thing. All the many saints are one bride. Are we one bride today? In a sense we are, but we may still be holding on to our concepts and opinions that damage the one accord. We are still in a situation in which we need the Lord's rescue, the Lord's recovery. I am afraid that a number of us are still under the negative influence of Christendom. We all have to realize that today the Lord is going on and on to fully recover us and bring us fully out of Christendom. The Lord desires something fully in the spirit.

The book of Revelation is a book of the Spirit and the bride. The church is something absolutely in the Spirit. We need to turn to our spirit and stay in our spirit. In the spirit we are one. Nothing is as important or as strategic in the New Testament as the oneness of the believers. The Lord Jesus prayed that we all would be one (John 17:21). Some maintain that they want to be scriptural, but in their exercise to be scriptural, they divide the saints. Nothing is more unscriptural than to divide the saints. It is better to have a whole man who is dirty, than a clean, dismembered arm of a man. The arm being clean may be likened to being "scriptural." Although the arm is clean, it is apart from the body and divided from the body. Some use scriptural things with an intention to divide the saints, but division is the most unscriptural thing.

Our need today is to be in the Spirit and in the Body, in the Spirit and in the oneness. We should care only for being in the Spirit and in the Body. This is what the Lord has been doing among us and with us throughout our history. Year after year the Lord has been gaining something because we are becoming clearer that the Lord's desire is absolutely a matter of our being in the Spirit and in the Body.

THE HELP I RECEIVED FROM BROTHER NEE
THROUGH MY PERSONAL CONTACT WITH HIM

In the previous chapter, I shared that I was called by the

Lord to serve Him in a full way on the day that I was saved. I gave up my job to serve Him full-time in 1933. Brother Nee wrote me a short note to strongly confirm my decision. After I gave up my job, I went to Shanghai and stayed with Brother Nee as his guest for about four months. During that time, I spent many hours with him in personal fellowship. He talked to me and helped me mainly in four things.

Helping Me to Know Christ as Life

First, he helped me to know the Lord's life. Before I went to stay with him, I loved the Lord and had learned a lot about the Bible, but my knowledge was mostly according to the letter. I was not that clear about Christ as life. When I contacted him, my eyes were opened to see life. When we came together, there was no form or rule to our conversation. His conversation with me was very free, and he would cover many different subjects. I considered myself as a learner, so I would always give him all the time to speak.

One day we were together, and Brother Nee was sitting in a rocking chair. While he was rocking back and forth, he suddenly asked me, "Witness, what is patience?" His question puzzled me because it seemed too simple. I knew that his question was more meaningful than it appeared, so I did not know how to answer. He asked me this question again. Then I said that patience is a kind of endurance by which one endures suffering, persecution, and ill treatment from others. He said that this was not patience. Then I asked him to tell me what patience is. He answered, "Patience is Christ." That sounded like a foreign language to me. I had never heard someone say that patience is Christ.

I asked Brother Nee to explain what he meant. But he would only say repeatedly, "Patience is Christ." I was very puzzled and bothered because I did not know what he meant. He just repeated again and again that patience is Christ. Eventually, I had to go back for dinner to the guest house where I was staying. When I returned, I did not eat well because I did not have the heart to eat. Then I went to my room. I knelt down and asked the Lord to tell me what Brother Nee meant by saying that patience is Christ.

Eventually, during that time, the Lord opened my eyes to see that Christ is my patience. The real patience is not our behavior. The real patience is Christ living Himself out of us. This was a great help to me.

Helping Me to Know the Initial History of the Lord's Recovery in China

Brother Nee also helped me by sharing with me about the first twelve years of the history of the Lord's recovery in China. Since I was not absolutely in the recovery during that period of time, he spoke to me in much detail about this history. At that time I did not know why he was doing this. Later I realized that he was laying a good foundation for me and building me up for my service to the Lord in His work.

Helping Me to Know the History of the Church

He also helped me by relating to me the history of the church, from the first century to the present century. My knowledge of the history of the church came mostly from Brother Nee's sharing with me. He presented the history of the church with its direction toward the goal of the Lord's recovery.

Helping Me to Know the Bible in the Way of Life

Brother Nee also helped me to know the Bible in a living way. The Brethren taught me to know the Bible according to the letter, but Brother Nee helped me to know the Bible in the way of life. Through all the personal times I had with him, he helped me in the above four aspects. I owe Brother Nee so much for all the help he gave me.

BEING BROUGHT INTO THE WORK WITH BROTHER NEE THROUGH TESTING

In addition to this, Brother Nee brought me into function by giving me the full way to participate in the work. I bore much responsibility in the church in Shanghai, and that gave me the best opportunity to learn. Before he put me into such a position, he tested me, and his way of testing was hidden.

One day he brought a bundle of letters to me, written by different persons with questions for him. These questions were about subjects such as the church, the church's ground, life, and the interpretation of the Bible. He asked me to answer all the questions for him in reply to all those letters. I told Brother Nee that I might not know how to answer some of the questions. He told me to do as much as I could. I eventually found out that this was his test. By having me do that, he found out how much of the truth was in me.

Not too long after my arrival in Shanghai, the brothers asked me to speak to the saints in a conference in the second hall; at that time the church in Shanghai had two halls. Nothing exposes where a person is more than his speaking. When a person speaks, everyone knows where he is. I spoke for seven days. Brother Nee was not there, but he received a report concerning everything that I spoke. That was also a test to me.

Later, I was asked to speak in the first hall, the biggest and primary hall. The church had arranged to have a big gospel-preaching meeting, but no one knew who was going to speak. No doubt, many thought Brother Nee was going to be the speaker. I was delighted and happy to be able to hear a message and learn more about how to preach the gospel. About an hour before the meeting, a small slip of paper was delivered to me from Brother Nee charging me to give a message on the gospel that night. I had no choice but to speak.

That night I gave a message on John 16:8-11. Verse 8 says that when the Spirit comes, "He will convict the world concerning sin, and concerning righteousness, and concerning judgment." I told the people that sin, righteousness, and judgment are related to three persons: Adam, Christ, and Satan. Sin entered through Adam (Rom. 5:12), righteousness is the resurrected Christ (John 16:10; 1 Cor. 1:30), and judgment is for Satan (John 16:11). All of us were born of sin in Adam. The only way to be freed from sin is to believe into Christ. When we believe into Him, He is righteousness to us, and we are justified in Him (Rom. 3:24; 4:25). If we do not repent of the sin in Adam and believe into Christ, the Son of God, we will remain in sin and share the judgment of Satan for eternity (Matt. 25:41). These are the main points of the gospel, with which the Spirit convicts the world.

When I gave this message, I did not see Brother Nee in

the meeting. Quite a time later, we were taking a walk together, and he said to me that not many people could give such a message on John 16 concerning sin, righteousness, and judgment being related to Adam, Christ, and Satan. He encouraged me to go on in my pursuit of the truth. I was surprised to find out that he knew the content of my message. He told me that while I was speaking, he was standing behind me, behind the back door, listening to me. My preaching that evening in the gospel meeting was another test to me.

PARTICIPATING WITH BROTHER NEE
IN THE ONE FLOW OF THE LORD'S WORK

Later, Brother Nee made arrangements for me to edit *The Christian*, a magazine for young believers, whereas he would edit *The Present Testimony*, a deeper magazine on the spiritual principles of life. At that time he also decided to publish a paper containing church news. That paper was called *The News of the Churches*. He charged me to take care of that paper. He also put me into a position of bearing the full responsibility for the ministry in the regular meetings of the church in Shanghai. This was because his health was not good, and he had to rest much of the time. He spoke mostly in the conference meetings.

In 1934, after I had been in Shanghai close to four months, Brother Nee said to me, "Witness, we co-workers feel that you have to move your family to Shanghai so that we can work together. Bring this matter to the Lord, and see how the Lord will lead you." I took his word and brought this matter to the Lord. Then I saw that in the book of Acts there was only one flow, one current. It started from the throne of grace and went to Jerusalem. From Jerusalem this flow proceeded to Samaria and then to Antioch. From Antioch it turned westward to Asia Minor and Europe. The book of Acts shows that there was only one current of the Lord's move on earth. There is no record of any work which was outside of this current. When Barnabas separated himself from Paul (Acts 15:39-41), there was no more record of his work in Acts. After this incident, he no longer appears in the divine narration in Acts of the Lord's move in God's New Testament economy.

The Lord impressed me that the current, the flow, of the Lord's work in China should be one. If the Lord was to do something in the north, I would have to jump into the flow at Shanghai in the south. Then eventually the flow would proceed to the north from Shanghai. Based on this revelation, I made the decision to go to Shanghai to work with Brother Nee.

After he had a conference with us on the overcoming life of Christ, under his leadership, a decision was made that we co-workers had to go out to the major cities to spread the Lord's recovery. I was assigned to go to the north to work in Tientsin and Peking. I went to work there in 1936, while Brother Nee remained in Shanghai.

While I was working in northern China, I received a cable from Brother Nee, asking me to come to an urgent conference with all the co-workers. In this conference in January 1937, he released the messages that are now contained in *The Normal Christian Church Life*. One day during this conference, he was ill, so he charged me to give his message on Acts 13. He gave me all the points and I wrote them down. I did my best to share in this meeting, but I did it in an inadequate way.

Later the decision was made by the work for me to travel throughout the provinces of northern China to teach, if possible, in all the denominations. We felt that since the Lord had given us so much light, we should pass on this light to the denominations. I did much traveling until the Japanese army invaded China. At that time many of the co-workers went to the interior of China, and I joined them. It was there that Brother Nee released the messages on the normal Christian church life a second time. The first conference was not so adequate. In this conference he succeeded in releasing his entire burden.

At that time my family was still in northern China, so I had to return. Because of the invasion of the Japanese army, I could not leave my hometown. Thus, Brother Nee and I were separated for a time. I stayed in northern China, and most of the co-workers remained in the interior. Through my experiences in traveling and speaking to many denominations, I realized that there was very little result. That caused me to make a decision not to travel anymore. Instead, I would stay in Chefoo to build up the church there.

In 1938 Brother Nee went to England and stayed there for one and a half years. He was also invited to visit some of the Scandinavian countries. He returned to Shanghai in 1939. That summer he had a conference on the Body of Christ. I received a cable from him asking me to attend this conference. I brought four young co-workers with me to this conference in August 1939. Through this conference we received a vision of the Body of Christ.

In 1940 he began to have a series of trainings. During that time he also had a conference in Shanghai about every two months. Furthermore, he spoke every Wednesday evening concerning the Body of Christ and God's eternal purpose. At that time I saw the blueprint of the practicality of the church life. I took this blueprint back with me to Chefoo, and for about two years we practiced what Brother Nee had seen. This brought in a great revival.

Meanwhile, there was a big turmoil in Shanghai in 1942, forcing Brother Nee to stop his ministry. This rebellious turmoil and the persecution of the Japanese army caused the church in Shanghai to close down. While the church in Shanghai was passing through this turmoil, there was a revival in Chefoo with the practicality of the church life.

Later, I was put into prison by the Japanese army for one month. After I was released from prison, I became sick with tuberculosis on the lungs. The Lord brought me through this illness within two and a half years, and after the war I was invited to come to Shanghai in 1946. It was there that Brother Nee and I met together again. We had been away from each other for more than six years. Because we had not had any correspondence during that time, I was concerned about whether what we had practiced in northern China was right. I presented everything that we had practiced in those years to Brother Nee, and he encouraged me to bring the same practice to the other churches.

I began to minister in Shanghai again, and there was a revival there in 1947. Through this revival, as I have pointed out previously, Brother Nee's ministry was recovered. When his ministry was recovered, there was an even bigger, broader revival among us. Eventually, about eighty to one hundred saints attended a six-month training with him in 1948. After that period of training, the trainees went to many cities, spreading the revival throughout China.

In November 1948, Brother Nee had an urgent conference with us, the co-workers around him in Shanghai, to fellowship concerning the work. We needed the Lord's leading as to where we should stay in the coming days for the Lord's work. At the beginning of that conference, he said that he and the other co-workers had to ask me, Brother Lee, to go out of the country, and that all needed to bring this matter to the Lord and see how the Lord would lead each one of them.

By February 1949, Brother Nee had a second conference with the co-workers to decide that I, Brother Lee, had to go out of the country and that he and the other co-workers should stay. Two months later from his training center, he sent me a cable, telling me to come to him and to hand over all the responsibility to the local leading ones in Shanghai. I went to him and stayed for a few days, and then I was sent to Taiwan. That was in 1949 and was the last time I left mainland China.

Then in 1950 Brother Nee came out of mainland China to Hong Kong and asked me to go there to meet with him. I went and stayed with him for one and a half months. I told him how the Lord had blessed the work in Taiwan and how within about one year, our number had increased nearly thirty times. Brother Nee confirmed that I should go back and stay in Taiwan. While I was with him in Hong Kong, he told me that his burden for China was so heavy and that there were many churches still on the mainland that needed help.

While Brother Nee was in Hong Kong, the church there was revived. This brought in a new start in the church life in Hong Kong. He charged me to lay the foundation of the church service there in Hong Kong for the church's building up. He also made an arrangement for the publication work. The publications were always under his oversight. When he and I were in Hong Kong, he made the decision that there should be a bookroom in Taipei and a bookroom in Hong

Kong to publish all of his books. He himself would oversee the bookroom in Shanghai. He charged me to take care of the bookroom in Taipei, and he arranged for Brother K. H. Weigh to take care of the bookroom in Hong Kong. He said that all the books could be reprinted and that all three bookrooms would have a common copyright. Thus, we began to reprint all his books for the need in all the places outside of mainland China.

My time in Hong Kong with Brother Nee was the last contact I had with him. From that time we only received news about him in an indirect way through his wife. His wife, Charity, went to the Lord in October 1971 in Shanghai. Brother Nee went to the Lord on June 1, 1972 while he was still imprisoned.

This brief history shows how the Lord has moved among us. We need to continue to pray for the Lord's move and for the Lord's recovery on earth in this present time.